Jou[illegible]ys and Voices: The Power of Youth Inclusion

15 years experience accompanying excluded Youth, with many more years ahead continuing to promote global Youth inclusion

Together we can!

YOUTH 4 CHANGE
NETWORK

COPYRIGHT PAGE

For more information: catalysts@lp4y.org

Paperback: 978-2-37608-018-3

First Paperback edition September 2024

Edited by: Fatine Benabdellah, Gwendoline Paquier, Indah Sinaga, Manisha Chapagain, Marion Laurin & Sally Day

Cover image by: Morgane Lebruman featuring Manita Chaudary at the Green Village Nepal

Publisher: Youth for Change Network

Publisher website: www.y4cn.org

DEDICATION

To the World's excluded Youth who firmly believe in themselves and came to LP4Y centers (Bangladesh, Egypt, India, Indonesia, Lebanon, Myanmar, Nepal and The Philippines) to unleash their potential; also to LP4Y's partners and Catalysts, who advocate with us for Youth Inclusion.

CONTENTS

ACKNOWLEDGEMENTS

CONTENT WARNING

PREFACE

INTRODUCTION

CHALLENGES & RESILIENCE

HOPE & AMBITION

COMMUNITY & SOLIDARITY

DREAMING BEYOND

CONCLUSION

GLOSSARY

ACKNOWLEDGEMENTS

As we celebrate the collective effort poured into *Journeys and Voices: The Power of Youth Inclusion*, we are deeply grateful to those whose support and dedication have made this work possible.

Our heartfelt thanks reach to the incredible young people whose voices and experiences are the heartbeat of this book. Your resilience, courage, and passion have been a constant source of inspiration. It is through your stories that we are reminded of the transformative power of inclusion.

To the many organizations and advocates who have been on this journey with us over the past 15 years, your unwavering commitment to promoting Youth inclusion has been instrumental. Your work in supporting and empowering excluded Youth globally has laid the foundation for the narratives shared here.

A special thank you goes to Catalysts worldwide, whose expertise and insights have enriched this project. Your dedication to creating a more inclusive world has been a guiding light throughout this endeavor.

Thank you to Frances Valadji, who kindly shared her comments and encouragement to ensure the pages are translated appropriately and cohesively, respecting the voices of our authors.

To everyone who believes in the power of Youth inclusion and works to make it a reality, we dedicate this book to you. Together, we continue to forge paths of opportunity and equity for Young people around the world.

And to John and Laure, thank you for 15 inspiring years of opportunity for growth, development and achievement.

With deep appreciation and hope for the future.

CONTENT WARNING

This book contains content that may be distressing to some readers, including but not limited to:

- Extreme poverty
- Discrimination
- Substance abuse
- Sexual content
- Mental Health Issues
- Child abuse
- Death and Grief
- Harassment

If you or someone you know is struggling with any of these topics, we encourage you to seek support from local services or international helplines such as Befrienders Worldwide.

www.befrienders.org

PREFACE

They are named Venus, Yara, Sohagi, Bhima, Manon or Aulia. They come from Myanmar, Philippines, Lebanon, France or other places in the world. They are one of the 52 brave young women and men, sharing here the stories of their amazing lives, the personal challenges they often have had to overcome, but also the dreams they have. With sincerity and passion, they open up their hearts by sharing their deepest feelings, which have sometimes made them sad, but simultaneously makes them hopeful for the future.

None of these stories will leave you unscathed.

By listening to each of these young women and men, you will undoubtedly be often speechless and bemused by the immensity of challenges they often have had to overcome. But I am also convinced that, like me, you will find a lot to reflect or learn from, on the meaning of words such as trust, belief, confidence or generosity. How can life take a completely different turn, for the better, when suddenly you start to realize that you are capable of amazing things. That's the entire story of Life Project 4 Youth; by bringing together women and men, they share stories and feelings, learn from each other, grow together, and commit to reach for their wildest dreams with energy and confidence.

Once you read these stories, they stay with you forever!

INTRODUCTION

In the quiet expanse of the night sky, where darkness mingles with the brilliance of countless stars, we find a reflection of our collective journey. Each star, a distant point of light, tells a story of its own, one of distant dreams and the enduring spirit that propels them across the vast universe.

Imagine, for a moment, that each story in this book is like a star in the night sky. From the bustling streets of India to the tranquil hills of Nepal, the vibrant communities in the Philippines to the dynamic corners of the USA. Each chapter illuminates the path of those who dared to dream and persevere. Each story within these chapters shine brightly, highlighting the journey traveled by motivated Youth, committed partners and energetic Catalysts from the LP4Y family.

At the heart of our narrative stand LP4Y alumni, the STARS, whose light embodies the strength and dreams of all who have contributed their voices. As they guide us through the stories of perseverance, hope, community and visionary dreams, they become more than a symbol — they become a guiding star in the ever-ending night sky, reminding us that each one of us has the power to shine and inspire.

As you turn these pages, let your mind wander to the sky, where the light of each story merges into a radiant constellation. Each tale contributes to a greater vision, a radiating display of collaborative power, creativity and passion.

CHAPTER 1: CHALLENGES & RESILIENCE

It is in the face of adversity that the true measure of strength is revealed. This chapter looks at the multitude of obstacles faced by excluded young people, from economic hardship, to social stigma. It explores the resilience they demonstrate in the face of these challenges, highlighting their unwavering determination to overcome obstacles. Through powerful testimonials, we discover the strategies employed to cope with these difficulties and the essential role played by Catalysts in providing support and guidance. This chapter bears witness to the unbreakable spirit of those who refuse to be defined by their circumstances, showing how they transform challenges into opportunities for growth and empowerment.

An Open Letter to a Mother
Lorene Tonati - Country Coordinator - LP4Y Nepal

Maman,

Three years! We never thought I'd be away for so long. Three years missing you, missing family reunions, but also three years of learning and of working out how to exist and grow on my own.

When you and Papa dropped me at Paris Charles de Gaulle Airport back in 2021, I was heading for the first time to Nepal; the birthplace of Buddha. I was younger then, maybe braver too, and hopeful and trusting of my skills and my qualities. And I was so happy and confident I would make a difference. As you know, since I was little I have wanted to change this mad world into something better. As a child, I thought it would happen through my spying skills (which I still hope haha), and back then, to do it as a committed member of the workforce. Yet, at that time I was full of insecurities I couldn't even name, probably because I wanted to appear confident in the face of your stress and concern for me. We said goodbye - who knew for how long? We didn't know that it was the last time we would see this version of ourselves. Because, Maman, there is no doubt that 3 years later, I am no longer the same person as I was at 24. So to me, the one word to describe LP4Y's experience is "changes". Let me walk you through some of them.

For the first time, I understood the power of collaboration and how the combination of people with different skills, yet all SO motivated and determined, could create a great impact in society. A society where too often, everyone is defeated by the size of the challenges. For three years, I worked closely in Nepal with 25 amazing Catalysts from Nepal, India and France. And together, we trained 735 Youth. At the end, 73% of the graduates found jobs. Said like that, it's just data, but the life trajectories of these Young women have taken a turn, forever. This is called change.

Generosity is one of the values I experienced. From the meals we shared all together every lunch and dinner, to those we took at the houses of the Youth when we met their families and discovered the conditions in which they lived, food played a major part in bringing us together. I also found generosity in the sisterhood the Youth demonstrated towards each other. I remember Nikita Tamang, a Young mother taking the training in the Training and Development Center Kathmandu during the winter in 2023, who publicly took the mic to congratulate and appreciate the determination and efforts of Kamala Doli (also a Young mother at the TDC, and a widow), who had worked until 2AM that night to rehearse again and again the presentation of her life project plan. Kamala didn't know how to write Nepali, and barely spoke when she arrived, but she rocked that presentation. Witnessing Nikita's generous act of kindness in acknowledging Kamala's hard work brought about a change in me.

Finally, I could describe all the important skills I developed through the handling of my mission of Country Coordinator, from leadership to management skills, public speaking skills to report writing... and I would say these are necessary to the values that got stronger: I believe more than ever in people, in our capacity to change our society. It is a strength to know how to rely on others and work together. To me, this is what LP4Y is: a workshop to make individuals and communities stronger, a place that believes in people's potential, especially that of the Youth, to become changemakers.

So yeah, Maman, I am about to come home, but I am no longer the same person, and somehow, I just love it.

With love,
Lorène

A better life and education for her children

Y. Amutha - Training and Development Center - Chennai, India

My name is Y. Amutha. I was born on July 25, 1993 in Puducherry, Union Territory of India. I was born as the first daughter to my parents Arumugam and Laxmi. I grew up in Tharamani, a town in Chennai city of Tamil Nadu. I studied my primary education in a government school in the same town.
After that, due to family circumstances, we shifted to Govindhasami Nagar, another place in Chennai. I completed my 10th grade in the nearby Mandaveli government higher secondary school. My parents were daily wage workers. It means that they were employed and paid on a day-to-day basis with no assurance that they will have a job the following day.

Something happened during that time that turned my life upside down. My parents used to get into arguments very often. One day, their fight went too far and both of my parents attempted suicide, which resulted in the death of my father.

After that trauma, I was forced to discontinue my education and went to work in a sweets manufacturing company to take care of my mother and younger brother. During that time, I fell in love with a person who is now my husband. I told my mother, but because of caste differences, my mother and relatives were against our wedding. I married my husband against my mother's wishes.
My husband has been taking good care of me since then. Despite the financial problems in his family, my husband never left my side and took good care of me. After 1 year of marriage, we were blessed with a baby boy. Yet, neither his side or my side of the family accepted us. No one from both of our families has helped us during our tough times. We somehow managed to run our family with my husband's salary alone.

After 3 years, I had a baby girl, but sadly we lost her as soon as she was born. This pushed me into depression, but with the good care and love of my husband, I was able to get back to my normal self. Two years after that incident, I was again with child, and gave birth to a baby girl.

After that, we were struggling financially even more. This is when I learned about LP4Y through one of my acquaintances. I got into LP4Y with the hope of getting a better job and providing my children with a better life and education than what I had. My husband has been supporting all my decisions and is still a major support to pursue my desires.

What did I learn in LP4Y?
I joined LP4Y on July 26, 2023. During the first month, I did not understand anything and did not know how to speak in English. During the second month, I started to understand English. During the third month I eventually started to speak. After that, I learned public speaking, team organization, and many other skills. I discovered many underlying skills of mine. I got to know about how to make a resume. I also learned about interviews and how to sit for an interview.

I really feel proud of myself for all the things that I learned and achieved in LP4Y and I am really grateful and thankful for the opportunity.

A Journey of Strength and Growth

Venus Rosario - Youth - Payatas, The Philippines

I was very young when my parents separated. I know my mother cheated on my father, but I didn't understand what that meant at the time. Sometimes, my mother would take us to fast food places with her lover, but I didn't know what it meant, so I kept quiet. My mother was often angry with my father because she worked while my father took care of us. I knew my father really loved my mother. One day, my mom said we could go back to the province, and she would stay in Montalban. My father agreed because he trusted her.

When we arrived in the province, we lived in our grandparents' house because we didn't have our own. After a month, my father decided to build a small house in the backyard. He enrolled us in the elementary school nearby. Since we were not financially stable, my father decided to send me to live with his cousin because he couldn't afford to send me to school, but his cousin could. I started living with my aunt, who sent me to school, bought me school supplies, and sometimes sewed clothes for me. I felt comfortable there, but my siblings did not. They often went to school without snacks, so I gave them mine every day.

The kids at school bullied us, saying we didn't have a mom and that our mom didn't like us. There were times when my younger siblings' classmates called me because my younger sister was also being bullied. I once saw boys in her class force her to eat a ball of paper, which broke my heart. Months later, my brother lost his right eye in an accident. He didn't tell us, and we thought it was just sore eyes. When it didn't get better, my father took him to the center, which said we needed to bring him to the hospital. They said his right eye was damaged and needed to be removed to save his other eye. It was hard for us, but we agreed to the operation.

When my mother heard the news, she visited us in the province and seemed worried. After the operation, my brother felt better. My mom decided to bring us to Payatas, Quezon City, where she lived. We didn't know then that she had a new boyfriend. My father didn't know my mother had cheated on him. When we arrived at my mother's house, she introduced her boyfriend to us. At first, I thought he was just a friend, and my mom said he was our uncle, so I thought he was one of her siblings. When I got older, I realized my mother had cheated on my father and didn't let him visit because she wanted to hide her affair. My father had to meet us at fast food places because my mother wouldn't let him come to our house. Sometimes, my mother taught us to lie to my father to get more financial support and to cover up for her boyfriend. During this time, I was very angry with my mother. Instead of teaching us good values, she taught us how to lie to our father and sometimes to other people.

When my mother decided to send us to school again, I was scared because of the trauma from our old school in the province. On my first day of school, I was very nervous and thought my classmates would hate me like the kids in the province. But I was wrong. I made a lot of friends, and one of them invited me to go to their church. I said yes, and every day after school, we would go to church. When I got home, my mom always thought I was flirting and hanging out somewhere else. I explained myself to her, but she didn't believe me and hit me every day because of it. I loved going to church because I felt like God was protecting me and loving me there. Even after my mother beat me, I felt that the church was my safe place. I felt loved there, but at home, I felt like no one loved me. My mother always said mean things to me, like my teacher and classmates did before. I was very angry with my mom, and I felt like I didn't want to forgive her. She was always kind to my siblings, even when they were disrespectful to her. My brother didn't respect me as his older sister, and my mother didn't care about that. I promised myself that if my mother got older, I would never take care of her because she always beat me and didn't love me.

When I started high school, I started entering into relationships to find the love I couldn't get from my mother or family. I always sought love from other people. I promised myself that if I had my own family, I would never let my children have a broken family. I started escaping in the middle of the day to meet my boyfriend. I thought that if my mother always thought I was flirting or being a whore, even if I wasn't, I might as well do it because she already thought that way about me. I had several boyfriends and failed relationships, but I always promised myself that I would never cheat. In my third year of high school, I met the father of my child. He was the only guy I introduced to my mother. My boyfriend always came to our house. One day, he said his mother planned to go to the province for good, and he would go with her. I thought he would leave me, so we planned to run away to his mother's province. When we were about to go, my mother's boyfriend saw us and didn't let us leave. He called my mother and the barangay officials because I refused to go home and wanted to go with my boyfriend. They used force to stop us, and we ended up at the barangay station. After talking, they made us sign an agreement. I agreed to stay at my mother's house, but that night, I gave my mother my bag and still went to my boyfriend's house. I decided to stop going to school and start working after that.

I started living in my boyfriend's house with his parents and siblings. At first, I liked living there, but after a few weeks, I felt like I was just a maid. After my boyfriend left for work, his mother always made me do all the chores every single day. His mother and sister didn't help me at all. I washed the clothes of his family members and even took care of his niece. I didn't say anything because I was scared they would be angry with me. So, I decided to find a job so I wouldn't have to do all the chores every single day.

At first, I was very happy because I had my first job and my first paycheck. I was a hardworking person and very dedicated. I always told myself that if I saved money and worked hard, I could go back to school. But my body became exhausted, and I got sick because I have to stand for eight hours and even though it's lunch we still have to prioritize the buying customers even though we are already eating as long as there are customers we must stop eating just to assist customers and since the restaurant is open 24 hours there are also replacements We work at night and when my replacement is late, I often work overtime but it is unpaid. So, I decided to quit and find another job. I applied as a saleslady in a small store. Unlike my first job, this one paid much less, but I kept going because I didn't have a child yet. Even though the salary was small, it was okay because it covered my own expenses.

I worked there for just three months because COVID-19 came to our country. The government declared a home quarantine, and no one was allowed to go outside. Every food stock we had was limited. The government distributed food packs so we could survive even without work. Months passed, and we were still in quarantine because of COVID. I got pregnant with my first child. I felt so happy even though I was planning to go back to school, even if it was homeschooling. Months later, I gave birth to a little boy. When my son turned two months old, I got pregnant again with my youngest because of a lack of sexual education.

I chose to be a housewife and focus on my children. Now, my son is three years old, and my youngest is a baby girl who is currently two years old. I tried to go back to school, but I didn't have anyone to take care of my children while I was in school, so I didn't have a choice. When my father found out about my mother's affair, he stopped giving financial support to her. He said I could get the money to support my siblings and me. Months later, my father had a mild stroke. Thanks to God, even though he had a mild stroke, he could still move all his body parts, but he moved slowly. Because of this, my father stopped working and volunteered to take care of my children.

During this time, I met Life Project 4 Youth (LP4Y), which offers free six-month professional training and financial support to marginalized women like me. My father suggested I join. I had always dreamed of having a decent job, one with a contract, benefits, and good pay. So, I started going to the center. At first, I was very shy and nervous. I was not confident with my English and didn't have enough confidence to speak in front of people. But after months of training, I became more confident, especially when talking in front of a lot of people. They trained us to speak in front of others, and I became comfortable speaking in English, even if my grammar wasn't perfect. Despite this, I never heard anyone judge or mock me. Instead, they corrected me, and I really loved the environment inside the center. Being there for just six months was a great opportunity for me.

Because of this, I plan to become a member of STAR someday and support Youth like me. I am much more confident now in applying to different companies, even without a diploma. LP4Y taught me that a diploma is not necessary to find a decent job. You just need the skills and determination to get the job of your dreams. If you have confidence in yourself, the people you meet will also have confidence in you.

Even though my past was full of struggles and confusion, I found my strength. Through the pain of a broken family and tough times, I learned that love can be found in unexpected places. With determination and support, I realized that you can overcome your past and create a hopeful future.

Family reunion

Abrar Hassan - STARS - New Delhi, India

Hello, my name is Abrar Hassan. I grew up in a village called Ahmedabad which is in the west of India in the state of Gujarat, with all my family. When I turned 7, my grandmother took me with her to Mumbai to live with some relatives and we stayed there for 2 years. After this period we came back to the village and I had to live with my uncle and aunty. I stayed there for 2 years and was tortured by my uncle. In 2007, I decided to leave and go to Rajasthan. I traveled there for some time but I needed to find a job so I came back to my family in the village. When I returned there I felt that there was a lot of tension... At this time my way to escape was to start drinking alcohol and smoking drugs in secret. I got arrested in 2010 and the police sent me back to Gujarat near my uncle. I went there for a short time just before leaving for Bihar and finally got onto a train for Delhi.

I lived in New Delhi Railway Station for quite some time. To earn some money during the day I was a waste worker. During this period I started again to use drugs and to drink alcohol. After 5 years, when I was 20 years old, I heard about LP4Y. At first I was nervous because I never went to school and I didn't have any educational background. I followed the LP4Y program for 2 or 3 months but after I had a big accident that put me into a coma and paralyzed the right half side of my body. I stayed in the hospital for one and a half years. After my recovery I decided to join LP4Y again and finish my PTE, because I knew that it was a good opportunity for me. At LP4Y I learned English, some computer skills, business management and the most important thing: I learned how to control my emotions. At the end of the program I found a job as a salesman.

It had been more than 13 years that I didn't meet with my family because I couldn't find any good reasons to go back. But due to the Covid-19, I thought that family is one of the most important things so I took the decision to go back and see them. My sister got married and has 2 beautiful children, so I met for the first time my 2 nephews and my niece. I met again also, my brother and my parents and we are now all very happy to be back together.

My challenges at LP4Y

Kay Khine Yee Yee Thein - Youth - Myanmar

My name is Kay Khine Yee Yee Thein. I am 20 years old. I live in Yangon with my big family.

Now, I am in the Responsibility step. I would like to share with you how I faced my challenges in LP4Y. Challenges in LP4Y are harder than I expected. First of all, I want to tell you about my life before LP4Y. Before joining LP4Y, I was a homebody, staying in my comfort zone. I spent most of my time in bed, just using my phone. After finishing 10th grade and starting university (through distance), I had a lot of free time. My parents didn't allow me to go out or work, so I ended up spending most of my days at home.

I want to improve something but I know staying in bed doesn't make my future better. Before LP4Y, I was really interested in learning French and learning from Duolingo. I found out about this program from my friend from the church where I usually go every Sunday. I was really happy to come to the center. My grandmother expected a lot from this program. She is thinking I'm going to get a job from this program. I explained to her later it depends on my efforts. I have a big family so I have to provide for them. From my home to the center by bus takes around 2 hours every day.

On my first day of this program, I was shocked because the Coach and Youths were greeting each other in English and I was worried whether I could do it. I still have worries. After two days, foreign Catalysts came to the center. I tried my best to communicate with them. We did a lot of communication and activities. Mostly it is about our dream job and how to know our career.

Catalysts and Coaches helped me a lot with speaking English (e.g. Sometimes we laugh when we are doing something wrong. But Coaches taught us not to laugh while others are speaking English. We must encourage them. Not to rush in speaking English and to be calm. They trained us in speaking, like tenses and how to use modal verbs for our daily conversation. Because we have to communicate in English during the program. During training time, I learned how to use Google calendar, sheets and slides and how to manage my time.

From a home person to working with a team there were a lot of challenges. In LP4Y we have to work with teams. I have to communicate with my teammates. As a learning and development team we have to discuss a lot. Many different opinions and many misunderstandings. About community training, we have to think about which templates we're going to use and who will search for information about the topic. My teammates were very helpful to me personally and professionally. During my two-month time in LP4Y, I changed and improved some of my habits as well skills like flexibility and active listening to others, teamwork skills, management skills, and also improved self-esteem. Also I changed my morning routine, I have to get up early to go to the bus stop. Following the center's rules and regulations will improve my own significant habits.

After LP4Y, my long-term goal is to be a Flight Attendant. My short-term goal is to advance in English and to get a decent job, so a good salary and reputation.

Doodling my way out of poverty

Min Thant Htun - Youth - Myanmar

My name is Min Thant Htun. I am a freelance doodle artist and one of the Youth from LP4Y in Yangon, Myanmar. I faced a lot of difficulties to follow my dream and to come to LP4Y, but I am doodling my own way out of poverty!

I come from a small town named Kyaukpadaung in central Myanmar, so it was very challenging to live in Yangon at first.
Yangon is a developed city where there are numerous opportunities to pursue our dreams, but they are not accessible to everyone as living expenses are costly. You also need a strong network to have access to job opportunities. In my small town, I could not do anything about my dream: it is far less common to have art events in the

countryside, and finding a job in this field was impossible. Due to our country's situation, my father did not let me go to Yangon. I argued with him every night. Finally, seeing my strong motivation, he let me go to Yangon. Before letting me go, he told me: "*Whatever you do, you must have a purpose.*" I was very happy at that time and I was thinking about steps to make my dream come true.
When I arrived in Yangon, I had no place to stay. My cousin's sister offered to let me stay at her place and I have been living there since then. During the first two months in Yangon, I was lost. It was hard for me to communicate with other people and I had no money to buy art material, which is expensive. I could not afford it. I felt depressed and thought that dreams are expensive. I did not know how to pursue my dream. To buy material, I started working as an art assistant teacher in a private school for kids. I also started playing football in Yangon every weekend to relax and make connections. This is how I met Ye Ko Ko, one of the Catalysts who is working at LP4Y. I decided to join the program, wanting to get a decent job in Yangon.

I received my first 24 marker pens bag as a birthday present from my parents. I drew the pictures and sold them to my friends. But art material is expensive. Sometimes, when I cannot afford it, I borrow it from my friends.

MIN THANT HTUN

FREELANCE DOODLE ARTIST AND YOUTH FROM LP4Y PROGRAM IN YANGON

Challenges are still there even after joining LP4Y. It takes me about 1 hour and a half by bus to come to the center every morning and every night to go back home. I always miss my home and I face a lot of challenges, but I also learn a lot of things at the same time. In LP4Y, I learned how to use a computer for the first time. Now, I know how to use Google Slides and I have basic finance knowledge. I will work as a digital communication assistant after LP4Y. My long-term goal is to become an animator.

If you face challenges in your life, do not stop and keep going. You should try to accomplish whatever you decide to do no matter how many challenges you face. It will all be worth it in the end.

My new beginning

Glydel Ignacio - Youth - Manila, The Philippines

I am Glydel Ignacio, I am 20 years old. I live in Payatas B, Quezon City. My family does not belong to a higher class of society, but we can still afford to eat at least three times a day. I stopped my studies because of lack of financial support. I stayed in my grandmother's house with her son and daughter with my four siblings because my parents are separated.

In 2018, our neighbor introduced us to Life Project 4 Youth and because of the good opportunity, two of the family relatives became part of LP4Y (Fashion 4 Youth and PayataSport program). They had a great experience where they encouraged us to be part of LP4Y too. Before they graduated, another member of the family joined LP4Y and she started a joyful and great journey there (Fashion 4 Youth program). After they graduated in the year 2019, they started to apply to many companies and they had many choices to apply. So thank you very much to LP4Y!

In 2020, we also joined the Life Project 4 Youth. My twin sister first became part of the Fashion 4 Youth program, then I became part of the PayataSport program on January 28, 2020. It is a pleasure for me to be part of the program because I learned a lot, especially the things I never tried before like Volleyball. In my 20 years of existence, I never tried sports! So thanks to LP4Y, I can now play volleyball and not only play but teach also. I am very happy because I also learned the basic computer skills,

Google slide, keyboard symbols and also presentation and professionalism. What more for my remaining months? There will be more knowledge and skills to learn. I am very thankful to Life Project 4 Youth for having this kind of program. It makes the Youth better than they expect themselves to be.

During Covid, it was a big challenge for everyone because we were far from each other. We needed to keep the motivation, the eagerness to learn,

especially if this will take one month. We needed to find distraction in the house. So thank you again for the online training, exercises and activities that the Coaches make, because it helps the team to keep the knowledge, develop our skill and not to forget.

To all the Youth like me: Always bring your motivation with yourself. You will not reach your dreams if you do not aim high and keep going even when someone or something puts you down. All challenges will be solved, maybe not now but it will come at the right time.

Being a Catalyst: A shot of energy

Beauty Khatoon - Program Coordinator - Nepal

Why are there so many restrictions? Is it a crime to be a girl? These are questions I always asked myself, being the eldest daughter and given the community I was born and raised in. I am a curious person by nature, and always have questioned the "WHY" of any stereotypes and superstitions that have been always tried to put on me. This questioning mindset and a purposeful vision in my life, led me to become the first woman in my family to receive further education and to have a chance of a better life by choosing my career and the job I am passionate about.

Hello, my name is Beauty Khatoon. I am 26 years old, and I am from India, from the Do-ars border in West Bengal; a border that is shared by two beautiful countries - India and Bhutan.
I graduated with a BCA (Bachelor in Computer Application), and then I realized that I cannot be living just working with computers for a salary with no meaning, or adventures in life and after that I started finding the actual meaning of my life.
Working for two years in Bihar, India, in a remote rural area helped me to find answers to my questions. To explore more about my lovely home state and to explore multicultural diversity, I joined LP4Y as Green Village Integration Leader in West Bengal. I applied for the position of Coach but was offered Integration Leader.

I worked as an Integration Leader for two and a half years in India & Nepal, where I have witnessed the impact of Youth coming from difficult and vulnerable backgrounds and some of them have brought change and impact in their lives. I remember a Youth from West Bengal telling me, *"Coach I do not want to go back to life, I came initially before joining Green Village, I am happy NOW"*. This statement from the Youth touched my heart and made me proud of the mission I am doing. When you see Youths who started their journey from scratch and now doing amazingly in their life, doing decent jobs, it makes you feel proud, every time I get the message that change is possible in your life if you give effort and of course, if you come out of your comfort zone.

I still cannot believe that, in my life, it led to working with young people who have a growth mindset and eagerness to do a lot of things in their life. Coming from geographical and social exclusion, I relate to the Youth during the training, which makes me satisfied with the work I am doing. The beauty of LP4Y is to work with people from multicultural backgrounds, where we share different cultures, food, clothes, and mindsets with a learning spirit.

Professionally I grew wings, and lifted myself up. I got to do a lot of projects with different centers of LP4Y. Personally, everything with my family has changed, the people I know now are different from the people I was brought up with. It's a life-changing thing for me. They are proud of Beauty. And I am proud to be a Catalyst, they appreciate what I am doing in my life.

I am also one of the rare Catalysts who moved from a local contract to an international contract and this immense belief from the Organization boosted my energy & dedication. From the age of 13, where I was told to get married, to now, working in LP4Y is a big and difficult journey.

For me, if you want to do something in your life, the first step is to come out of your comfort zone, it needs to be your call. I am happy with what I am doing in my life, and want to keep doing this journey, where I am at my best, most honest, version of myself. I want to do the same as LP4Y is doing maybe I will succeed in replicating LP4Y pedagogy in schools, government organizations etc in my hometown to mobilize women and empower them, they have a lot of potential and change that they can bring to a society and Inshallah one day I will.

The shooting star

Manon Breguier - Coach - Cagayan De Oro, The Philippines

I am Manon Breguier, from the South of France. At the age of 23, I am lucky enough to be part of this wonderful organization, LP4Y. I had been chosen to become a Coach in the Philippines, more precisely in the southern part of the country, in the Mindanao region. Because yes, I am a southerner no matter where I live. But more seriously, I would like to tell you about the biggest challenge I faced during my mission.

So this story takes place on a warm April day, barely two months after my arrival in the country of smiles, as I like to call it. That moment marked my experience as a Coach, but above all as a person. And it left an indelible mark on me.

I had been at my training center for a month and a half and was starting to get to know my team well. Among them was Jezza, a young woman to whom I paid particular attention. She had never learned to speak or write. And despite the fact that one of the center's micro-companies is American Sign Language (ASL) training, she also had difficulty with this form of communication.

Given these circumstances, communicating with her was complicated. She was very sensitive and deeply kind. Me and my co-Coach, Gladys, tried to support her the best we could with her future life project. We pushed her to dream big as we do for all the Youths who join the center. She had just completed the six months of training and it was time for Jezza to receive her final LP4Y diploma and become the entrepreneur of her own life, the last stage of the program. We had scheduled her graduation for the weekend.

Three days before her graduation, on a Wednesday morning, Gladys came to me with the most shocking news. Jezza's mom had suddenly passed away. I had seen her mother 2 weeks earlier and she seemed in excellent health. I was therefore particularly surprised and shocked by this terrible news. Nobody deserves to lose a parent at such a young age. But it hurt us all more to know this tragedy affected the only person at the center who was not self-sufficient and who depended almost entirely on her mother. The whole team was very saddened by the news. We decided to support her and all be there for the funeral on Friday evening.

Obviously, I wanted to be there to show my support, but having lost my father when I was only 18, it was hard for me to attend the ceremony... However, when the time came, I went, accompanied by all the Youths from the center.

In the Philippines, the deceased are laid in an open coffin in the street and I wish I had known this information before I went. When I saw Jezza's mother's body, I was transported back to a time when I had promised myself I would never go again. Seeing another dead body was hard, because my father's death had traumatized me. I remained as strong as possible in front of the others, and supported Jezza the best I could. We all stayed at the bedside for about two hours.

As we were leaving, Bea, another young woman from the center, remarked how beautiful the moon was that night. Indeed, it was a full moon, so we stopped for a moment to admire it. Then a shooting star appeared. It was so big that its light almost blinded us. Then silence fell, and we all made a wish.

I saw it as a sign. A sign that I was in the right place. I was sure I belonged here, alongside these young people who were teaching me so much about myself, the world and life. A beautiful message of hope, even in this time of sadness.

I only needed someone to talk to…

Camille Ocubillo Manalastas - Green Village Calauan, The Philippines

Hi, my name is Camille. Let me share my story with you.
Before I went to LP4Y, I was lost. I had no goals, no plan in life. I wasn't able to finish college because of poverty. I had to work at an early age. Life was like an endless cycle of the same routine. I woke up, ate, worked, then went to sleep. Until my brother introduced me to LP4Y. After his graduation, I eagerly sent the requirements to Mathilde who was the Coach of the Green Village at that time.
I've waited months to be able to join Life Project 4 Youth. I remember my first day, I was so excited to learn new things. I remember the training, the relationship I formed with other Youths and Coaches.

LP4Y helped me a lot in boosting my confidence, I was very shy and unsociable but everything improved after. I didn't just learn to speak English fluently or master Excel. I learned the value of believing in myself and how I should visualize my success someday. I also learned to believe people telling me that I have potential.

The day of my last graduation came. I thought I was ready and confident enough to face the world again. I thought I was ready to step out of my comfort zone.

I was late and I was not able to come in time for my interview in CGI. I failed that day. But I refused to be a "tambay" or good-for-nothing. After a week, I looked for another job as a cashier in a small restaurant. At that time, I pitied myself a lot because I let the big opportunity slide. Until one day I got the good news that I would get another interview in CGI.

I practiced and practiced my interview; I made sure I knew a lot about the company so that I wouldn't fail again. Then after two months of being a trainee, I got the contract. I remember the sweet sound of the pen as I write my signature on my contract paper. It was the happiest day of my life because I got what I dreamt before. And I thought that was the meaning of success but life never ends there. It never always ends on happy endings like the ones we see in movies. Sometimes it ends because you want everything to end.

I became suicidal, I overthought people's opinion and ended up not getting enough sleep because of those things. I hurt myself a lot of times, I smashed bottles onto my head, I pulled my hair so that I would feel the physical pain rather than the pain that I'm feeling inside. I remember the night I was rushed to the hospital because of that deep cut on my wrist. A lot of people misunderstood me, they thought I was asking for attention. My family thought I was just broken-hearted. They never understood that I needed help. I only needed someone to talk to.

Sometimes people don't die from mental illness, they die because of stigma. Because no one understands how it feels like to wake up each day, finding reasons to wake up. Being mentally ill is hard, but it's harder when someone calls you crazy, or someone tells you to just be positive and then you'll get over it.

It's like telling a blind person to open their eyes so they can see.

I took this opportunity to testify to everyone of what being depressed feels like and how stigma makes them feel. So if you see a friend struggling to get out of bed, help them and encourage them to stand. We will never know if someday they ran out of reasons to wake up. And if you have a friend who struggles to sleep at night, talk to them and ask them if they are okay because we will never know how tired they are from fighting with their demons inside their head. And if you are the one struggling today, I hope you take care of yourself. I'm proud of you because you're doing your best and you're still alive today. If you need someone to talk to, we are always here and you aren't alone in fighting the unseen battles.

We are here to listen; I am here to listen.

You see, success is not about the type of job you get or how much money you earn.

Success is about your growth from each path you take and being the better version of yourself from yesterday.

I speak from my old self who died 3 years ago,
I speak for the people who died from suicide,
And to my friends who have existential crises.
I am Camille and this is my voice.

Turning Failure into Success

Lovely Joy M. Jimenez - Youth - Payatas, The Philippines

I am an independent and strong woman who has lived on my own since I was a teenager. When I was just 8 months old, my own mother left me for her new family, and although my father was around, I always felt alone. I have lived with my grandparents since birth, but they were often absent due to work. Sometimes, they took me to their workplace, even to the dumpsite, when I was 5 or 6 years old. Between the ages of 14 and 16, I worked as a housemaid, and I felt capable of living independently. I funded my own education through various jobs, even though they were not always respectable. I worked nights and attended school in the mornings, often sacrificing sleep. During my graduation, no one came to support me; I celebrated my victory alone.

Throughout my teenage years, I always felt alone and sought companionship everywhere, which led me to seek love from friends and others. At 17, I became pregnant, which was early, but I had no hesitation because my child brought a sense of completeness to my life. His birth gave me hope and ambition, motivating me to strive every day to support him.

When I saw a post from one of the Coaches at Life Project 4 Youth, I didn't hesitate to join. On my first day, I felt excluded, doubting my abilities compared to others. One of the Youth spoke to me, saying, "*It's part of the process. You're here to build your confidence and skills through training.*" It made me realize that I wasn't there because I knew everything; I was there to learn.

Day by day at Life Project 4 Youth, I faced challenges, achieved milestones, and learned valuable lessons. They helped me understand my worth regardless of my lack of formal education. They didn't judge my background but gave me a chance to prove myself.

I remember my first challenge at LP4Y: delivering a speech during a company visit to one of their partners, Concentrix. I accepted the challenge to boost my confidence and gain exposure to the corporate world.

They also gave me the opportunity to intern at a bank for two weeks, an experience I thoroughly enjoyed. Becoming a Youth at this organization taught me so much and contributed greatly to my personal growth.

Joining LP4Y changed everything for me. They helped me discover my capabilities and changed my perspective on life. Before LP4Y, I thought my only role was to be a good mother and that I didn't have the right to dream anymore. Now, since joining LP4Y, I have made significant changes in my life. I have allowed myself to learn new things and become stronger in facing life's challenges.

I am very thankful to be a part of this organization. I now feel valued and important because I made the decision to join. I remember my younger self who had many dreams to pursue. I didn't realize that *"sometimes it's the smallest decisions that can change your life forever."*

From Youth to Catalyst: A Journey of Growth

Yara Abdallah - Coach - Green Village Lebanon

I want to share my journey and experience with LP4Y in Green Village (GV) Lebanon, where I began as a Youth participant and grew into a role that has profoundly impacted my life.

When I first joined LP4Y, I was seeking guidance and support to become more responsible and independent. I wanted to learn how to create a professional CV, write a compelling motivation letter, apply for jobs and perform well in interviews. My goal was to prove to myself and others that I could achieve success on my own.

At GV Lebanon, I received training that developed both my soft and hard skills. During my time as a participant in the LP4Y program, I was also preparing for my final exams at the institute. I successfully completed my studies and earned a certificate in nursing.

As I entered the job market, I focused on nursing and healthcare positions. Despite applying for many jobs, including door-to-door applications, I struggled to find employment. After leaving the GV, I continued my job search and eventually found a position at a nursing home. However, the salary was low and the location was far from my home, making it financially unsustainable.

Throughout this challenging period, my supportive GV leader, Mona, frequently checked in on me. She encouraged me to keep trying and never give up. One day, Mona offered me an opportunity to become a Community Life Coach (CLC) at the GV for a month. I was overjoyed and immediately shared the news with my mom, celebrating the chance to give back to the community that had helped me so much.

My journey as a CLC began on October 26, 2023. Seeing my former Coaches and now working alongside them was a dream come true. My first Monday was a significant day, with Ghida (Coach) providing me with a thorough handover. Shortly after, we welcomed a new batch of Youth. Although I was a bit nervous, the experience was incredibly rewarding as I felt myself growing and gaining confidence.

Day by day, I learned and acquired new skills and qualities. I now understand how solar panels and generators work, how to handle maintenance tasks, and take on real responsibilities. While I am not a mother or sister to the Youth, I always strive to support and push them to reach their potential.

One memorable event was the E-Day, where I witnessed the incredible talents of the Youth at GV and TDC. They performed a theater piece on gender discrimination and unity and then we all danced the traditional dabke. The experience was challenging during rehearsals, but the final performance was worth every effort. It was a significant achievement, especially for the shy participants who gained confidence through the talent show.

Since May 2024, I have been Coaching Youth in the micro-company and I am proud of my growth in this amazing place. I continuously learn and improve, never hesitating to ask questions and broaden my understanding. Working with others who have diverse mindsets and experiences has been invaluable.

Additionally, being part of the GV community has been an enriching experience. The sense of belonging and support has been a crucial part of my journey. I have formed meaningful relationships and learned the importance of community life. It has taught me the value of collaboration, mutual respect and the power of working together towards common goals. This community has become a second family to me, providing encouragement and inspiration every step of the way.
Initially, I was anxious about my new role, but now I feel more comfortable and confident. My curiosity and desire to learn more about Coaching have brought me to where I am today. I am grateful for this journey and excited about the future.

Finding My Path: From Lost Dreams to New Beginnings

Min Khant Aung - Youth - Yangon, Myanmar

My name is Min Khant Aung. I am one of the Youth from LP4Y in Yangon, Myanmar.

Before I joined LP4Y, I didn't know what my dream job was and I lost my passion. In the past I dropped out from school and I didn't learn anything at that time. I lost my passion and I don't know my career and what my dream job is. I was trying to learn the Korean language, but it was not ok for me and I am not interested in that language. But I learnt because I don't know my passion and I was trying to find my career. But that was not working, I got depressed and stressed. That time was the worst time in my life. Within my family, I had many family problems and teenage problems. At that time I wanted to go away from my family and I lost my dream, which was to become a professional artist.
One day, my friend told me about community training for the LP4Y program. He told me I can join this community training. I was interested, so I came to the center and I joined the training.
That training was very fun and I was very interested in this program. I asked about this program, and the current Youths explained it to me. I decided to join. First day of discovery week, I was a little bit bored and my interest was a little bit lost. But I came on the second day also. That day was very different. I thought this program is very good for Youths. So I thought I should join this program and then I joined.

I got a lot of challenges at the autonomy step like communication, English speaking, using the computer and many other things. But I was motivated at that time because the Youths are very good at communication and all the Youths helped me. So I always come to the center and I am never absent.

I got a lot of experience from this program and I got a lot of knowledge about time management, saving money and managing money. The biggest change was time management, because I was always late to the center. The Coaches always talked to me to be professional and to manage my time and what the solution was to arrive on time. And I tried to arrive on time but I was late every day. That's why the Coaches told me, if I was in a company they would not allow that behavior and they would fire me. They told me to write a motivation letter and cut my allowance for the whole day. At that time, I understood and I tried to arrive on time the next day. That worked for me and I arrived on time that day. And then I was never late to come to the center and my time management was good from that time.

The training was very good for me and I got a lot of experience, knowledge and I changed myself to be a professional person and to be a good citizen. The LP4Y program changed everything for me. Now my communication skills, English skills and public speaking skills have improved. I am more confident and more professional than before. The LP4Y program impacted me too much and changed me. Now I am in a responsible step and I learnt many things from this program. This is the best experience for me.

Coach Aung Kyaw Oo said *"Stay in the Present and think about the Future. But don't forget the Past."*

Now, I am trying to go to the future, I discovered my passion and I already found my dream job. My dream job is to become a professional Artist. Now, I am going to my dream and I committed to myself to focus on that dream.

A calm sea has never made a good sailor

Romain Mailliu - Former Catalyst - Indonesia

Our center: a sailboat in the storm. Events follow one another like waves that we take in full force without being able to catch our breath. Sarah is gone but Fanette is back after ten days confined in a hotel. Fever, dizziness, headaches: she thought it was the coronavirus, I thought it was the coronavirus, you thought it was the coronavirus. It was not the coronavirus.

So our boat is taken over by the swell. Every wave is a concern, a jolt to consider. Not all of them are equally threatening, but they come from all sides. Boat? Storm? Wind and tide? Romain, have you lost your mind? Let's take a little bit of a break from that dubious metaphor.

These waves are the problems - let's say challenges - of young people who are evolving with the coronavirus. At this stage, there are usually economic challenges: Taufiq's father has lost his job, he is the only one who can bring back money to feed his family. Fikri's parents have returned to the village to flee the virus, he is now in the street. These challenges are added to our daily work. Toy can no longer come to the center because he has to help his grandmother to collect plastic bottles to sell them. Fami is going to give birth in 4 days and does not have enough money to give birth at the hospital. You get it, that's a lot of challenges.

In this hurricane, sometimes the most dangerous opponent is under the sea. A strong current causes us to drift and makes it difficult to stay on course. It wakes up especially in the evening, when night falls, and nothing seems to be able to stop it. This current is the continuous information about the coronavirus that attacks us day and night. Social networks, newspapers, television, e-mails, flyers, visitors: It is impossible to disconnect or to tell the true from the false. I feel like I'm being spammed, stunned by data that keeps falling on me endlessly. So I keep a few snippets of information, entered here and there, and sometimes I share it with anyone who wants to hear. Without meaning to, I imagine that I add a layer to the general incomprehension.

There's no sailboat without wind, and no storm. Friend one day, enemy the next, the wind is a bipolar character. Its role is decisive when one undertakes adventures at sea. Its breath can carry our boat to more prosperous horizons or break it down and send it out to feed the fish. Blizzard is sometimes a morning caress, it's confusing. When the mistral wind rises, the sails blow up and the sailors sing. This wind is our family in France. They play a decisive role as the virus claims more and more victims. This is the reason why a volunteer decides to leave the ship to go home. The family, like the trade winds, is an inexhaustible source of energy. Sometimes it only takes a phone call to tame the waves or to tear the sails... "*Are you going back to France? Congratulations on your commitment! Are you safe? We are proud of you. We miss you...*" The words of our families fuel our fears and joys. We must know how to detach ourselves from them without distancing ourselves.

The wind is the shadow of the storm: when it rises up against the sun, it loses its hostility.

Fighting one challenge at a time to become Coach at the GV Bangladesh

Sohagi Akter - Coach - Green Village - Bangladesh

I am Sohagi from Bangladesh. I am 21 years old. I am doing my Bachelor of Science 2nd year in Lalmonirhat government college of the zoology department. I live with my parents, and there are five members in my family.

Now, I want to share my life journey along with some dreams. I always wanted to be self-reliant. Because I did not want to depend on my family. That's why besides studying, I tried to do something more. I have always believed in myself. But my life journey was not very easy, because I faced many obstacles in fulfilling my dreams.

Most of the people in the village believe that one should not get married at an older age. What happens after studying so much? The community always told my parents to get me married off. But I am very proud of my parents because they always supported me.

One day, I heard about LP4Y from a Rangpur Dinajpur Rural Service (RDRS) team member. He told me that "*LP4Y is a computer training center*" and it's international. After hearing about LP4Y, I was interested. At first, my father did not allow me to come to Green Village, Bangladesh. But finally he agreed to let me go and complete the training.

I took professional training from LP4Y Green Village Bangladesh from September to December 2022. I was team leader of the Digital Center Micro-Company from Batch-8. First, I went through the computer training that I was told about and after a few days I realized it was more of a professional training center. Before coming to the Green Village I did not know about professionalism. Then, day by day, I gained some knowledge about it. Also, I developed some soft skills like leadership and good communication with the team and Catalysts. As well as some basic English & computer skills. I had some challenges in the first week like learning to adapt with so many people around me and dealing with time management. But after one month, I overcame my challenges.

From the first day, my dream was to be a Catalyst. At that time our Community Life Coach was Sharmin Sultana (Medha). All the time I was trying to follow Medha. That's how I know about the CLC mission. If

Medha had vacation time, I was training to do group tasks to support her.

After I finished my professional training. I got an offer for the Community Life Coach position from February 2023, it was a great opportunity for me. At first I was thinking *"How will the other Catalysts be? Am I going to get support from them?"* But after a few days they are always trying to support me. If I say I cannot do this, they tell me *"Yes you can"*. I got a lot of motivation from them. Before I had less motivation. But now I am full of motivation and self-confidence. Also, now I know who I am.

After joining as a Community life Coach, I had few challenges. On the first few days some Youth treated me as Youth or as a friend. Also they did not want to do evening activities. But I was always trying to make them understand why it's important for them. After a few months, I finally succeeded in getting them to understand. This was my best moment in the Green Village Bangladesh!

Since January 2024, I have been working here as a Coach for Digital Center & Sustainable Development micro-companies. My goal was to be a Coach, so that's a big achievement! My neighbors feel proud of me. Also my parents are very proud of me for my achievements.

Overall, I realize nothing is impossible. Everything is possible if you have good motivation. Always stay positive! Allow yourself to think deeply. Don't be demotivated. Remember your goal. You will succeed one day!

CHAPTER REFLECTION

At the end of each chapter, you will find a space intended to respond to all four notions. Use this page to draw, write, think.

How have you adapted or changed in response to challenges?

Are there areas where you need to further adapt or shift your approach to be more resilient?

CHAPTER 2: HOPE & AMBITION

In the face of a multitude of struggles and obstacles, the flame of hope and ambition continues to burn in the hearts of many young people.
Through a series of captivating and inspiring stories, we explore how these young people, driven by hope and ambition, manage to transform their aspirations into tangible successes. Their stories are a testament to the power of perseverance and the incredible potential that lies within each individual. We'll hear about their journeys, the obstacles they overcame and the triumphs they achieved. Illustrating how their unshakeable will has led to profound personal and professional growth.

You have to jump and see what happens!

Lucie Dubert - Green Village Leader, Nepal

I joined LP4Y with a commitment to work alongside the poorest and most excluded people. I arrived in India, full of convictions, ready to launch the first Life Project Center (LPC) in Bangalore. With me, my partner, Géraldine.

We first met in Nantes, as we both prepared for departure. We know nothing about each other, yet here we are, both embarking on an extraordinary adventure.

Together, we discovered colorful temples and cows wandering in the middle of the street, spicy curries and rickshaw rides. Very quickly, Sheraldjin, as some Indians call her, became my closest ally. On arrival in Bangalore, we immediately get to work. Our goal is to find a site for the new center and to start training young people as soon as possible.

As we meet with local actors, we come to understand that poverty here is much less visible than in Calcutta, Mumbai and Delhi where LP4Y teams have already set up several centers. Many Bangaloreans we meet are surprised by our quest. For them there are no slums in Bangalore; we should be looking at another city for our project. Poverty in this booming city, which has become the third largest city in India in a few decades, is hidden, stifled, ignored. This embarrassing segment of society, the segment that LP4Y wants to bring into the light, well, we had to search hard to find it.

In the end, we decide on Devarajeevanahalli (known as Djhalli) as the site for our new LPC. Djhalli is a slum of 100,000 people; enough to prove wrong all those who question the existence of extreme poverty in Bangalore. This invisible district is also excluded from the rest of the city because the community is predominantly Muslim, hidden in plain sight in the largely Hindu state of Karnataka. Although they have been here for several decades, the inhabitants speak Hindi and Urdu, the national language of Pakistan, but rarely Kannada, which is the local language of the state.

When you arrive in Djhalli, the transition is brutal. The beautiful paved road gives way to a rush of rickshaws. The glass skyscrapers disappear on the horizon and little by little the minarets of the mosques appear. The call of the muezzin drowns the incessant noise of horns. Here, there are no gated communities with guards at the entrance, instead children run about freely. Most houses in the neighborhood have four concrete walls and a tin roof.

Perhaps to compensate for the gloomy interiors of these small dark cubes, the exteriors are brightly painted by the owners. Some streets are colorful mosaics, brightening up the black burqas. There's a juxtaposition of contrasting images: at the corner of a street, a small church with a blue bell tower stands next to a bloody butcher's shop; cricket bats in hand, the youngsters noisily play cricket on a rubbish-strewn pitch. The electricity supply is precarious and yet most people have a television. At the market, the foul smell of fish stalls in the sun gives way to the scent of fresh coriander two meters further on. I see the diversity of this place, and struggle to interpret what I see. The more I see, the less I understand. It seems you can live in the most basic house in the neighborhood, but that doesn't mean you have no education. You can own an entire building, and yet still wash your dishes in the street. For the moment I can't tell who is rich and who is not. There is lively confusion all around me.

One thing is certain, however: here, men reign supreme. They have beards rather than mustaches and apply kohl around their eyes. Their teeth are stained red from chewing betel quids, and their appearance sends shivers down my spine, reminding me of so many threatening Jafars! No polite smiles; just stern looks that seem to question what a white woman is doing here. I feel uncomfortable, out of place. I too would like to be able to slip into a burqa... Integration is going to be complicated. The Djhalli district is indeed a slum: the poverty is blatant there, exclusion palpable. The faces are marked with life's violence. So, what changed my fear into wonder, my pity into gratitude?

LP4Y's purpose is to support vulnerable excluded Youth, to help them find and keep a decent job (with a contract, fixed hours and salary, and if possible medical coverage and social benefits).

Each center set up in Asia targets a different population, selected after analysis of local issues. Some centers are reserved for young mothers, others are dedicated to street Youth, some even to prisoners.

We decided that the Djhalli Center would be for young women. To publicize the project in the neighborhood and meet the Youth likely to form the first team, we go out to meet the inhabitants, dressed in our lovely LP4Y polo shirts.

Despite having imagined this moment many times, having completed my training course, and really looking forward to finally meeting these young people, it's not easy to get started.

Knocking on doors, introducing yourself, making contact despite the language barrier. Confronting our fear of the unknown. I'm worried about disturbing them, being too intrusive and being turned away. I walk without really knowing where I'm going. I wander through small alleys. The further I go, the more entangled the houses become. I take an alley to the right and find myself in the poorest area of the neighborhood. There's corrugated iron wherever I look. Families have limited and irregular access to water but this morning, the fountains are overflowing.

The unreliable pumps transform the street into a paddling pool. The women, in flip-flops and night wear, their hair gleaming with coconut oil, wait their turn to fill their bowls. Some are already vigorously scrubbing clothes; others busy themselves soaking pans from the day before. In short, it's not the moment for introductions ...

I catch the eye of a young woman hanging out her washing,

I bravely move towards her, jabber the few Hindi words that I have learned and ask her age. But she smiles at me, uncomfortably, and goes back to her business. Failure. I continue on my way without much confidence. I am overwhelmed by everything going on around me when I hear:

— Which country ma'am?

I turn around. There's a man sitting on the steps of his house, arms folded; the jaded spectator. He doesn't seem very busy.

— France, I reply.

— Aaah, France! Mbappe!

I take this as an opening and explain the project to him.

— I am looking for young women aged 17 to 24 who do not go to school and who do not work.

He looks at me and pulls a face. I smile as best I can. He gets up nonchalantly and as if in a supreme effort, calls out to the busy women. Some, focused on their chores, barely pay him any attention, but others listen closely.

— My cousin's sister is 18, no work, no school, she can come?

At last - some interest!

— Of course, of course, where is she?

In response to my enthusiasm, the woman gets up, leaving her washing bowl and decides to guide me through the maze of barracks.
Off we go! A lively procession joins us: a few women who have chosen curiosity over laundry; the Mbappe fan; and a crowd of children.

All of us in search of the cousin's sister in question. I am no longer in unknown territory. As I listen to the kids calling *"sister, sister!"* I feel more as if I'm part of a big family reunion. In less than five minutes, I feel like they've adopted me. I'm barely inside the house before a baby is put in my arms. After a few dozen selfies taken with each of the neighbors, my apprehensions are a thing of the past. We talk, we laugh about our difficulties in understanding each other. I allow myself to be swept from one house to another; at each one the hostess offers me something: if I'm lucky it's tea, if I'm unlucky, a revolting sickly-sweet soda. I meet some young women who will be able to join the program but, more importantly, I immerse myself in this new environment. I start to feel good here.

In just one afternoon of outreach, my perspective has changed. I no longer approach the neighborhood as a potentially hostile or dangerous environment but as my new home that contains more "Indian moms" than I could have imagined. Over the months and thanks to the local inhabitants, this atmosphere will become more and more familiar to me. This neighborhood will be my anchor. And I can go further: those terrifying bearded men will become solid partners for the creation of the center. There will be Afzar, our main contact, always available to put us in touch with motivated young adults. In respect of his motto: *"First eating after meeting!"* We eat an obligatory biryani before each meeting.

There will be Asif, the owner of the building, and Siddiq who will renovate it. I can laugh now about my scary first impressions.

The women will open their doors to me and explain their daily struggles. Their generosity and radiant smiles will almost make me forget the garbage dump next to where they live. Above all, there will be the Youth and their families, who will invite me with open arms to share their daily lives, their ups and their downs.

Strength in Simplicity: A Journey of Hope

Bhima Palungwa - Entrepreneur - Nepal

Hi my name is Bhima Palungwa. I am 23 years old. I am currently studying BA.LLB and I am a 4th year student. I also have a job in a law firm as a Receptionist. I am here to share my journey. Thank you for giving me this opportunity.

I am from a small poor family and a lot has changed from where I started to where I am today. I want to give credit to everyone who made me who I am today.

What do you call delicious food? For me salty vegetables and rice are delicious foods. I never asked for anything, even when I don't understand things. I learned to deal with my circumstances in life. When I was a child, my father was not with me; even if he was with us, either he used to get angry or was not in touch. My dad mostly worked as migrant labor in the Middle East and comes back to Nepal to see my family once in a while. So, that is why the relationship with Father is on and off. It is because of the consequences of poverty and long-distance relationships within family members. I grew up in my mother's parents' house. There were only 4 of us: me, my mother and my grandparents.

My mother said that she enrolled me in a government school by selling chicken at 50 rupees. She works as a laborer at the house building site. She could not afford the school boarding fees with that income. The money from her wages was enough to pay for my food, clothes and pay for my tuition fee. My family never stopped me from studying, they always encouraged me to study.

Our house is made of mud and we had to put buckets in the house in the rainy season. No matter the difficult situation I was living in, I never felt we were poor. Maybe I'm just happy with what I have. In Class 2, this question was asked during the English exam: "*what is your father's name?*" I did not have the answer. Perhaps there are few people who don't know their father's name. I didn't think so at that time. I wrote my friend's father's name.

When I was in class 3 and about 9 years old, my father, after a long time, came from a Middle Eastern country — where he was working as migrant labor — and I was glad that we all moved into one house — father, mother, siblings, and grandparents — before we were living in a maternal house with maternal parents.

However, after a brief period of time together, my father had to go abroad again to cover my school fees and, more importantly, to earn money as we planned to purchase property for a house. And, after a year of my father's earnings, we were able to buy a piece of land where we had previously resided (eastern Nepal). But again, we were short on funds to build a house because my father brought a limited amount, which we used to purchase land.

We are thus forced to remain in the same home with a leaky roof.

Regardless of a difficult family situation, on the one hand, my family (mother especially) kept hope and gave the utmost love, and on the other hand, the more love I had, the more responsibility I had.

To fulfill my parents' wishes, I wanted to build a house. So I always thought of becoming a lawyer, engineer, and doctor only. Because in that profession there is both power and money. I didn't think about how I could. I just told myself I have to do it, there is no other option. By the time I passed 10, I had thought that I would study law because I liked to speak for others. I studied law in Class 12.

I had to go to Kathmandu to do my bachelor's degree. I was happy and wanted to tell my father. But happiness did not last long. My mother and grandmother gave their land to their grandchildren in relation and it was the land that my father and I were expecting to build a house one day. When my father found out about this, he stopped talking again. It was not my fault or theirs. They wanted to help others and thought they would return it. It was okay for my father to be angry as they gave the land without discussing it with my father first. This greatly affected my studies. But I didn't stop. I thought that *"Whatever happens, I will see."*

My mother gave me money from a piggy bank, which is 5K NPR (about 30€) and my grandparents gave their old allowance, a total of 25K (nearly 170€) and I left my home for the first time. I took the entrance exam and I was selected but I am worried how I can pay such a big amount. That time I had to pay 87K (585€) and I didn't have that much money.

I remember those relatives who say "*You go, we will help you with big hopes,*" but they only give excuses. So again, I called my parents and I shared it with my grandmother. She is the only woman in my life who understands what I want. She always encourages me to think big and dream big. So, she forced my grandfather to give me money because he had money. He sold slum area land and sent me 1 lakh (about 670€). I got admission in law college. Because of my grandmother I got the chance to study.

Sometimes later I have to get citizenship so I went to Taplejung (Eastern Nepal) to my father's home (an ancestor place). It had been a long time since he returned from abroad but he did not want to talk to me, and it really hurt my feelings. To make him talk to me again, I told him we got the land back. But it was a lie that brought more complications in my life. Some time later my father returned. I panicked. What should I do now? Because of my lie, I could not be happy about his return. I felt guilty. I asked the person on our land to return it to us, but she just ignored me and made excuses.

I decided to tell my father the truth, and he understood. We filed a case against the people occupying our land, and we got back the land. Without his support I don't know how I could have handled things. My father started stressing about my study because there is no income source and my study is not complete. He had more than 5 lakhs

(3,400€) when he came from abroad. I convinced him to come home and build a house because grandmother's situation is worse because of critical health issues, and she still was hoping to have a good house to stay in.

Now ready to build a house, he invested all the money. It was important to me to see my grandmother happy because she is the world to me. It gave me the motivation to just fight with a lot of situations.

After that, I started seeking a job but I started to doubt myself. I had fear of judgment and no confidence. But 1 day completely changed my life. My sister shared a post on social media about LP4Y training. I was just curious to know what that is and called. The lady who received the call had a polite and sweet voice. I asked her how I could join the training center. She said: *"You have to come tomorrow."* So I decided to go there because there is a living allowance also and training where I can gain experience and money also which helps me for my daily life also.

I decided to move to a slum area also because before I lived in a hostel and there I had to pay 10k monthly. With financial problems, day by day it's hard for me to pay. My father was against it but I convinced him. At the beginning, I was afraid of living there because many people who live there use drugs and alcohol. But I started to live there. LP4Y allowance helps me to live there.

In LP4Y, I can openly express my opinion without judgment. I just feel confident. There, I see many types of people who are learning from base and some are experts. Everyone is treated equally. The best part I feel is collective guidance. That time I learned a lot of things. Which helps me for self-awareness. I am always grateful for LP4Y who helped me to achieve my goal.

I completed 6 months in LP4Y. During that period, all Coaches and Catalysts helped me. After that, I searched for a job in a law firm. Before LP4Y, I tried, but they rejected my application. And they offered me only NRS. 5,000 monthly (about 35€). But later, thanks to LP4Y, I knew my worth, and I upgraded my skills, so the same law firm offered me a job in a receptionist position with a decent salary, i.e., 110€ per month for 5 hours of work per day. So, I am successful in achieving my short-term goal (in a law firm as a receptionist).

The training helped me a lot. I now know how to talk with people with confidence. Before LP4Y, I didn't know how to print things but now I know how to do it. So I confidently print the papers and make files. The small, small things I learned in LP4Y help me to have a clear vision. I am happy I got a job related to my field. LP4Y training made it easy to work there. My journey is still ongoing but I am clear about my objectives.

In my difficult time, LP4Y supported me a lot, I am always grateful. I got the job and now I am independent. I pay my room rent, my food bill, all things. So today I am here because of LP4Y. It's the best platform to grow yourself.

Confidence is the key

Matthieu de Romblay- Project Leader Partnership - The Philippines

When I first came across LP4Y, I immediately wanted to commit and become a Catalyst. The challenge of accompanying Youth from slums towards a decent job was simultaneously in line with my deepest beliefs but also the skills I was able to develop during my previous experiences.

I therefore came to Manila in February 2019 to start my mission as Project Leader for Partnerships. In each country, LP4Y builds bridges between the slums and the decent world, the world where everyone has a roof over their heads, several meals a day and access to healthcare. The partners work with us to build these bridges - these are the organizations, the associations, the companies which accompany the training and the job integration of the Youth. My role was to develop new partnerships and strengthen the existing ones in the Philippines, Vietnam and Indonesia.

I had the good fortune to witness the joy of the Youth as they discovered companies. I witnessed their contagious joy at every hiring. I recall one Youth from my center, Angelito Mendoza, who was unable to contain his pride at being recruited by CGI and who left the center running to announce the good news to his relatives. His brother, impressed, could not believe him: for him, such jobs were reserved for college graduates, so for a Youth who hasn't finished high-school, it was uncredible! These outbursts of happiness are part of the most memorable moments of my mission. These memories remind me every day that when we work together, we can realize extraordinary things.

As I spoke to Angelito and others during my mission, I realized that the main factor of exclusion of young adults is not the lack of skills; many of them are smart and motivated. What actually stands in the way of the Youth is the distrust of the companies, their reluctance to take the risk of meeting unusual profiles. To be successful, we all need someone who reaches out to us, who believes in us, and only once we have that trust, we can prove ourselves. I have witnessed managers and directors of companies who dare, who take the risk of trusting these young people and who reap the benefits of their decision. A Decathlon manager testified that in a few years, he would no longer remember the figures for his store, but he will remember that he accompanied Mary Jane JC as she found her place in the team, and of the commitment, the joy, the motivation she brought to the group.

But sometimes, giving that trust is not enough. Some of the Youth quit a job that seemed to suit them perfectly. I was particularly frustrated by these missed opportunities, by these young adults who don't take their chance, perhaps the only chance of their lives.

I remember Marissa Tadlog, who after going through a long application process to join a hotel, did not show up on her first day of work.

Similarly, Angelyn quit an ideal job to spend more time with her family after only a few weeks. Living through these moments of discouragement, I felt I understood an essential part of being a Catalyst. It is not only a matter of supporting the Youth as they seek a job, working on the short term. It is also a matter of helping them build self-confidence, and helping them to realize they have a place in a world from which they have always been excluded.

You have to be patient, humble, and admit your helplessness when faced with certain situations when some Youth leave the program before the end, or when others give up what seems to be the ideal job.
Our role is to always be there, to look out for them, to believe in them when they no longer have the energy to believe in themselves. And it works.
Each month, the Youth who have left the program return and those who missed an opportunity come back more motivated than ever to find the job which will change their lives.
Marissa finally got a job as a receptionist in the ZenRooms hotel chain, and Angelyn got hired a few months later in Sodexo. She now has a salary that allows her whole family to live.

That's right: for me, trust and confidence are the essential elements.

I also gained self-confidence during the year: confidence in myself to dare to ask for help from the community, to ask partners to commit to inclusion. As my mission progressed, I became convinced that, contrary to what I thought, a vast majority of people are ready to help. Almost everyone has untapped natural reserves of altruism. Some people give time by offering training to the Youth; some make donations to finance a project; and a few just take five minutes to connect us with one of their friends and these five minutes will result in the hiring of the Youth and an eruption of joy in the slums of Manila. When I talk about giving, it's obviously not one-sided. At LP4Y, we say that there is not one way: there are not the ones who give and the ones who receive on the other side. Youths, donors, partners, Catalysts: we all benefit a lot from this experience and I would recommend it to anyone. It was an extraordinary year for me.

LP4Y is my Oasis

Puja Dhungana - Coach - Green Village Nepal

Namaste. My name is Puja Dhungana. I am a young woman of 22 years old from Balthali, Kavre Nepal. I am a high school graduate. Despite personal challenges, I joined LP4Y's Green Village on December 8th, 2020. Ever since I heard of this project, I had made up my mind to be a part of it and nothing could deter me from my decision.

I was born and raised in a small village in Nepal. Dreaming big was not an option for me. In fact, I was scared to dream big. I was busy with chores and

other responsibilities but I was always hungry for something more. I was hungry to better myself. To learn more and to do more. I always questioned myself, is this all I was meant to do? To be born, raised and die in a small village?
Something inside me always told me that I am meant for something big. I had a dream but I didn't have the support or means to fulfill my dream. I didn't know who to turn to and who would support me to achieve what my inner self told me I was capable of.

In time, I came to know about LP4Y and just like that I made a decision that I must join the Green Village. I knew I would have to leave home, my comfort zone, my family and go to a new city and be on my own. I am going to be honest, this scared me a lot. As I rode on the bus, I knew I was leaving a part of me behind. My heart grew heavy and weary just at the thought of leaving home and stepping into the unknown.

Throughout the entire journey to Green Village, my mind was consumed with questions. Was I making the right choice? Is this going to be worth it? Questions I had millions, but answers I had none. All I knew was my heart was filled with hope with every kilometer towards the Green Village.

As I ascended the stairs of the Green Village, I could see that this place was special. It was no more just me with my doubts and questions. I saw that there were Youths like me there. I left home only to realize that the Green Village was my new home. I left my village only to realize the Green Village was a small

village on its own with all the Micro-Economic Initiatives within it.
I left my family but I was in the presence of Coaches who love us so dearly. I felt like I had everything I could dream of. The fear of oblivion had now passed. I felt like a traveler in the desert who found an oasis. I knew I had to be molded like raw clay and now I had found the cast.

With time now I realize that you've got to "*dare to dream.*" Through LP4Y I have learned that I have to believe in myself. I know that life doesn't always go according to plan but after coming to LP4Y I have learned to be prepared for any challenges in life! With LP4Y, I have learned practically to be calm when challenges occur. I am a new "me" with LP4Y and I feel like it has given me a new perspective to look at life. LP4Y has opened my eyes to really recognize my capabilities and work on them. I know with determination and hard work, I can lead the life I desire. I am the main actor of my life and I am capable of helping others in the journey of life. I had limited expectations from this project but I have received much more than I had anticipated. Truly, the knowledge I learned in LP4Y will be very useful in my personal and professional life. I cannot say the same for my formal education! In school, I learned to pass the test but in LP4Y, you learn by doing, you learn about your skills, qualities and moreover your capabilities. It's difficult to express in words how thankful I am towards LP4Y for giving me the chance to become a better person by working on myself.

I came empty handed and am leaving with so much learning and for that "*Thank you*" would be a small word. One thing I can promise is that I will cherish my time here and help others by sharing the learnings I received.

After 3 months of training, I became STARS Club president and I learned a lot throughout this journey. Today, I am a Catalyst myself. There is a saying: "*Choose a job you love and you will never have to work a day in your life.*" I didn't even realize it has been already 5 months that I am working with LP4Y as a Catalyst. Maybe that's how I relate to the saying that I mentioned above.

When I was a president of the STARS Club, I used to give testimonies to the Youth and I always used to tell them that your past really doesn't matter, what kind of background you belong to. What matters is what you want to bring in your life and what you are doing with your life right now.
One day, I was talking with the Youths about motivation. Someone asked me what my background was. I smiled and said "*I also belong to the same background as yours.*" She asked me again: "*What did you do after 3 months of training?*" I replied that I did group agriculture, taught in school as a teacher and volunteered in RCF Nepal as well. For women's economic welfare, I worked as president in a women cooperative. She asked me again "*How did you manage to do all this in such a short period of time?*" and I said "*It's not about time, it's all about energy and self-motivation.*"

Talking about my mission, Community Life Coach is such a unique and beautiful mission. I am enjoying this mission a lot. Day and night, I'm able to observe the Youth with empathy. The growth that I see in them inspires me to be an even better person. When I see the Youth, it makes me realize that I am living a meaningful life. Many Youths tell me that I am their inspiration but in reality they are the ones who inspire me because I work with them, I learn with them and I grow with them.

One day I was feeling sick. It was very cold in Godawari on this day. Some Youths knocked on my door and asked me if I was fine or not because they wanted to do yoga with me at 5:15am in the morning. When I saw them standing outside of my door in that cold, my sickness faded away. They do English class with me every day after dinner even though they are tired. It gives me pleasure to see them trying their best.

I feel proud to work as a Catalyst in LP4Y. I feel proud to work for the Youths from different backgrounds of Nepal. I feel proud to be such a person who can put themselves in those young women's shoes and relate to them. I feel proud to be able to observe their growth. I feel proud that I can say to all the Youth *"never stop trying."*

From a former Youth to a STARS Club President and STARS Club President to a Catalyst who's held multiple positions, I am grateful to be able to grow with LP4Y. I am grateful towards life, the amazing team of Green Village Nepal, the Youth and myself also for always being dedicated and passionate. I am really excited to do more and explore more.

As a Catalyst in LP4Y, I finally feel like I have started the journey on the path which I vowed to myself when I was 13, when I told myself I want to be a useful person for society. Still a lot of things need to be done but I am proud of what I am doing now and where I am going.

Margaret: ready to face challenges to achieve her dreams

M. Margaret - Training and Development Center - Chennai, India

My name is M. Margaret. I am 22 years old. I was born on April 25, 2001, in Chennai city, Tamil Nadu, is where I grew up, I have a younger brother and we live with our parents. My parents' names are Mariyadass and Matilda Mary. They have both been working since the ages of 13 and 15 respectively. My father is working as a watchman in a residential apartment and my mother is a domestic worker. My brother has a Diploma in Electrical Engineering but he is currently jobless. Even after doing a one-year apprenticeship at Chennai airport, it is tough for him to find a job.

I completed my schooling through a scholarship in Chennai. For my brother's and my higher education, my parents had to borrow money from others to pay the tuition fee. Afterward, they struggled a lot to repay that money.

I am the first person to graduate from my family. I am a Bachelor of Science and Education graduate, a 4 year integrated course that enables one to become a teacher in math and sciences in schools. But places are limited and at the end of my course, I didn't get a job.

During my childhood, we lived in a small house that was built using dried coconut leaves. On rainy days it was tough to live there, as it would leak whenever it rained. The area we lived in was not that safe as there were a lot of vehicles around, so me and my brother used to play inside the house only. Our childhood was not that simple. I remember that one day, the corporation authority demolished our house and we had to stay in the street for almost 2 days after that. At that time, my brother and I were very young and I cannot remember the details, but I remember that I was scared, and thought why is this happening to us?

After that, lots of things happened in our lives, we faced many challenges in our day-to-day lives. When I was studying 9th grade, we got allotted a house in Ezhil Nagar through a slum clearance board. Life was not really easy for us in Ezhil Nagar, we faced different kinds of problems: financially and with relatives. At that time, my mother needed a major operation after which she had to rest for a whole month. My parents used to argue and quarrel a lot, which affected the overall well-being of my family, and added a lot of mental pressure. In addition, I too had health problems; polycystic ovary syndrome, kidney stones and low hemoglobin levels.

I eventually started to understand life and people. In these few years, my family has seen different phases of life. We learned about people around us, whom we can count on and whom we cannot. In all of this, money and people played a big role. These were the toughest years of our life. It took some time for us to recover from that psychological pressure. The Covid lockdown period helped us heal slowly. We spent more time together and got to understand each other.

After this period, everything was going fine. When I finished college, my mother had another major operation. Her uterus was fully removed, which finally helped her to heal. However, the financial problems remained.

I came to LP4Y in the hope of achieving something big and I really hope LP4Y would be my first step towards that. My mission is to help my parents and give my family a better life.

I want to be someone who faces challenges and inspires people to achieve their dreams. I want to have my own identity and I want to create my own individual identity. I always think big, because I want to achieve big. The only person I want to prove I am capable of great things is myself. I want to prove to myself that I am capable of doing anything and everything, and I know the biggest and toughest opponent one could face in their life is themselves only. I know that, to achieve something big one needs to work hard, and I am ready to work hard, ready to face challenges and ready to learn new things.

After joining LP4Y I discovered that I have so many hidden skills and talents, so I want to improve and develop those. I can already see that my skills are improving. I feel more confident and I can see some improvements in my personality as well, for which I am happy.

I really hope LP4Y will be my first step towards my dream and I hope through this I can give my family a better life and I really think I will be successful. I hope to learn more in LP4Y and I want to make my parents proud. Lastly, I may be born as an ordinary person but I am sure I will not die as being the same ordinary person. Let's hope for a better future!

Noemie's journey at LP4Y

Noémie Cabantous - Catalyst - The Philippines

At 27, I made major changes in my life. May 2020, in the midst of the pandemic, I needed liberty, optimism and I had a strong desire to get involved in a cause close to my heart: to show that everyone has their place in this world and can aspire to a brighter future.
This is why, despite people telling me *"you're not 20 anymore"* and *"coming back will surely be difficult,"* I joined Life Project 4 Youth, an international movement dedicated to the social and professional inclusion of young adults.

In the 77th episode of Nouvel Œil, Victoria Guillomon asks Arthur Auboeuf what advice he would like to give young people today. Arthur suggests we approach it like this: Just close your eyes and imagine yourself old, bent, tired, gazing into the distance and saying to yourself *"I wish I was 27 again - I wish I could go back."* Then open your eyes and feel that surge of energy, pushing you to dare, explore, be free to finally say to yourself *"before being that old, I will first be that young!"* To feel there, alive.

When I joined LP4Y at 27, I had 1,000 opportunities to feel alive:

- Alive when sharing profound, funny and often totally unpredictable moments with LP4Y Youth, their families and my colleagues in the slum areas of Dhaka and Manila.
- Alive when bursting into tears when the lockdown in Manila came up, canceling

most of the actions I had worked on for months with partners in the Philippines.

- Alive exploding with joy while reading the text message from Wendy, an alumnus, telling me that, after 4 years, she had finally secured her dream job at Decathlon The Philippines, allowing her to get out of poverty.
- Alive when seeing Rhamzi's look when he realized, a few days before the end of his professional training, that his discretion was his best asset and that the other Youth appreciated his trustworthiness in team projects.

Today, I'm almost 29. I learnt that everything is possible, and that our experiences are what make us special.

At the end of this month, my LP4Y mission will be over. I will go back to France, to start a new project that fits me 100% and that I never could have imagined 1 year ago!

Chasing Clouds with Youth

Aulia Lutfie - Ecosystem Developer - Indonesia

I was born in a small town in Central Java, Indonesia, where most people seek work abroad as domestic helpers or blue-collar workers. From a young age, I dreamt of soaring among the clouds, inspired by watching *Doraemon Japanese cartoons* at a neighbor's house. Growing up in a family that faced economic hardships, especially during Indonesia's financial crisis, with only my father working as an elementary school teacher, I learned the value of perseverance early on.

Living in poverty and being a victim of both physical and mental bullying were significant parts of my childhood. Indeed, poverty can diminish one's stature and marginalize a person. However, it also strengthened me, instilling a belief that I could change my circumstances.

Beyond academics, I realized that change comes through action, so volunteering became my gateway to shifting perspectives. I learned that sharing is not just about money but also about lending a helping hand; our lives complement each other.

My big dream of stepping foot abroad motivated me to pursue grant sponsorships through volunteering programs. The visa application process required me to travel back and forth between Kendal and Jakarta, a journey of over 415 kilometers.

As I traveled by train into Jakarta, I was struck by the sight of shanties, slums, people sleeping under bridges, and overcrowded semi-permanent settlements amidst scattered trash along the railway. This reality is completely different from the grandeur of Jakarta, often praised for its high minimum wage that attracts people from rural areas to migrate to the city.

In 2021, a few months after completing my volunteering program in Germany, Syaiful Islami Ramadhan, a former Coach of the Training and Development Center Jakarta, invited me to work with LP4Y Indonesia. I was thrilled, yet apprehensive. North Jakarta, particularly Tanjung Priok - Cilincing, has a notorious reputation for being a slum area with high crime rates, poor sanitation, and a close proximity to large garbage dumps. Despite these concerns, Syaiful's explanation of the program captivated me, and I knew I wanted to be part of this mission.

In August 2021, I became a solo Coach due to COVID-19 restrictions, delaying the arrival from France of my partner Coach Fanny for about five months. Not yet accustomed to the city, and easily moved by the harsh realities of life in the capital, I sometimes felt overwhelmed. Dealing with excluded Youth, trying to maintain professionalism while not interfering in their personal lives, was challenging.

The first three months were incredibly tough. Seeing pregnant Young women arriving at the center with bruised faces from domestic violence or sexually abused by stepfathers, victims of poverty's cruelty — evicted, sleeping in carts, burdened by family debts, broken homes, drug-addicted parents, struggling to survive — their tears often left me crying alone in the bathroom. Stepping into their shoes, I realized everyone has their story, and it hurts.
But the essence of their journey always ends with hope for change. Their hopes are simple: a bed to sleep on, two meals a day, education, a home, conversations with parents without financial

demands, and happiness. For me, success is relative — even eating twice a day is an achievement. Their determination to progress makes me grateful that simple dreams can drive action.

Remember my dream of seeing clouds? Now, I see clouds with the Youth. Clouds symbolize freedom: the freedom to choose their own lives, access equality, break free from limitations and abuses, become their best selves, and most importantly, break free from poverty. As their Coach, I witness them crafting their path towards those clouds.

At the beginning of the program, the Youth are unable to make eye contact, unsure what they want in life, feeling lost. They slowly transform into individuals who are more confident and driven. Who says this journey is easy, especially for those starting from scratch? Imagine a young adult walking from the slum through the capital city of Jakarta, with just a CV in hand, under the scorching sun reaching 37-40 degrees Celsius, with barely enough money to sustain his or her life. Every tear shed and every drop of sweat is a part of hope.

Seeing Youths transform to gain employment, sharing their life advice and stories of how they found happiness, I believe that life evolves and I remain optimistic. I learned that everyone has blessings and can be a divine instrument in blessing others' lives. When a Youth chooses to leave an abusive relationship, forsake home to pursue dreams, and stand on their own, it's a triumph, proving even a small candle can offer hope in darkness.

Each success story — escaping abuse, rebuilding lives — is a testament to resilience. For me, the presence of LP4Y is one of the most crucial factors in creating an ecosystem that encourages Youth to dare to dream. It convinces them to step forward and ensures that someone believes in and supports them to secure decent jobs and better lives. Furthermore, it's not just the Youth who grow, but everyone involved — like myself, Catalysts and partners.

Thank you, from the depths of my heart, to John and Laure Delaporte and LP4Y's visionaries who prioritize enriching Youth's potential over mere charity. Thanks to LP4Y, thousands of Youth dreaming of seeing a sky full of clouds, including myself, have found their paths.

Believe in the power inside you!

Jiselle Rabaca - STARS - Payatas, The Philippines

Hi Everyone! I'm Jiselle Rabaca. 'm 23 years old and a mother of 2 kids. I work as a Junior Analyst at CGI in The Philippines and I graduated from the Life Project Center Payatas in March 2019. I am also a Grade 11 student and class president as well as the Secretary of Quezon City STARS club.

At a young age, I became a mother but always held on to the hope that I would be able to finish my education after giving birth. Unfortunately, I was held back by financial challenges. At a certain point, I experienced depression and was filled with anxiety over how my kid's future will be.

Then an opportunity came for me to start a small document printing-business using my basic knowledge of computers. It was during this time, while I had little confidence that I could step into that door, that I came to know about LP4Y and the wonderful opportunities the training could bring.

In LP4Y I became very comfortable with my co-Youth and Coaches and surprisingly, with myself. I went through several mock interviews and company visits which allowed me to explore and experience how it is in the corporate world – the way people actually dressed and spoke – which were all just in my thoughts before. I was able to intern in Messy Bessy where I shared my stories in different LP4Y events. In my job search, I would have 3 company interviews in 1 day and would be told I would get an update on the interview result. That's how it went until I was interviewed at CGI Philippines on June 18, 2019.

They appreciated how I demonstrated all the learnings I gained from LP4Y, the way I shook my interviewer's hand, my body language, my effort to practice my English communication skills and how I expressed my eagerness to learn and get out of poverty to secure my son's future. That's how I became part of CGI. It was not easy when I trained for my job – reading invoices in different languages and analyzing figures which all required attention to details. But after years of doing the job day-in and day-out, and being in the corporate world, I noticed how much I grew and how much of my life has changed. I realized I am now living my simple childhood dream.

When I was little, I envied my brother because his birthday was December 31st and there would inevitably be a celebration where there was delicious food and our family was together – because it was New Year's Eve. On my birthday, which is December 30th, we didn't even have a picture of our family being together and there wasn't even a small cupcake for me. So, when I had my son, I wanted him to feel that his birthday was something to celebrate. I consider it one of my biggest achievements when I was able to throw parties for my children and that I was able to spend on one of those parties even while I was recovering from my eye surgery. Those events, among other things, make me feel proud that I have grown so much and continue to grow. I do believe that there is nothing impossible for me as long as I have the will to continue.

My personal experience with the guidance of LP4Y tells me how much being part of the working population positively impacts the lives of excluded Youth and how the working population also benefits from the relationship. Excluded Youth usually have the stronger drive and determination to work hard in order to forge a better future for themselves and their families. These are the kind of workers companies need and should nurture because we are eager to prove ourselves and be assets and when given the opportunity we become very loyal members of the company.

Every single person here is not the same. But we are all looking for the same things to help us achieve our goals. We all need guidance, encouragement, openness and the opportunity to be productive members of society. I am personally grateful for LP4Y and CGI Philippines for providing all those things that I carry with me while continuing my journey towards the realization of my dreams. But on top of that, I am grateful for myself. Each of us working to make our dreams come true should be proud of ourselves because we take the first step, the initiative to learn, and we keep taking steps no matter the challenges and we kick the doors open and create opportunities for ourselves. I MAKE IT HAPPEN. EACH ONE OF US MAKES IT HAPPEN. Believe in the power of YOU.

From Happyland to Singapore

Monette Tenedero - STARS - Tondo, The Philippines

I am Monette Tenedero, a young mother who used to live in Happyland (biggest slum in Manila). I still remember how I dreamed during my younger age and suddenly changed when I got pregnant at an early age. I thought that my life was over and hopeless but when I learned that there is an organization named Life Project 4 Youth, I feel fortunate and even my perspective on life changed!

LP4Y provides qualitative training like exposing myself to actual management of business, purchasing and making a product to sell. I feel that day by day the training boosts my confidence and this becomes my strength.

I am thankful that LP4Y gave me a chance to extend my knowledge by attending company visits with partners and universities. By attending this training, I notice that I develop so many skills like professional behavior, communicating in English language, managing the team and operating our micro-company that help me in different situations.

I dreamed of working for a good company to finish my studies but it was difficult for me to achieve it while supporting my three children. *"HOW CAN I PROVIDE A BETTER FUTURE FOR MY CHILDREN?"* This question kept on circulating in my mind and kept me to challenge myself, to continue and fight for my dreams!

When I was hired in Decathlon in 2017, I felt very grateful to this company because they gave me a chance to have a decent and stable job! This chance that LP4Y & Decathlon gave me changed my personal life and professional life.

At first, I thought that it would be easy for me to work while taking care of kids but I was wrong! Decathlon Alabang is the first branch in the Philippines and I am the first from LP4Y who got hired. I felt pressure at first but they supported me a lot in the professional aspect. I learned during my training in LP4Y about the importance of attendance. Despite almost 3 hours of travel to work in Alabang, I was never late. I am grateful to the Catalysts that accompanied me and Mrs Nadege because they ensured my emotional wellbeing that prepared me for who I am today and not just my professional path.

I worked for Decathlon Philippines for 6 years and throughout these years, I could see that my life is improving. I now had savings for my kids, a house in Antipolo, meaning that I would not need to think of our safety anymore (Happyland is prone to fire). At the same time, things remained difficult as I got separated from my partner and became a single mother! While working too hard, I was not able to focus on my children, which hurt me a lot as a mother but every time I took days off, I would make sure to give my full attention to them!

I am now working in Decathlon Singapore as a Sports Leader! I believe that working hard with a goal will lead you to a brighter future and that you can learn to develop an entrepreneur mindset! Do not lose hope for your dreams and keep fighting, that is my advice to the Youth!

Me, Manisha

Manisha Katwal - STARS - Green Village Nepal

Namaste!

Everybody has their unique hidden talents, which needs a proper and perfect environment to grow and the Green Village has helped my light to burn brighter and to grow in the form of Professionalism.

First of all, I am very much grateful to this project who has provided me a golden opportunity to share about me and my story and here's where my story begins.

It's me, Manisha Shrestha. Formally known as Manisha Katuwal while being at GV. I am from Chaubise Dhankuta, and currently residing at Godawari, Lalitpur.

My journey at LP4Y began when the mobilization team visited CPCS Godawari, where I was staying. I got to know about the LP4Y project, which increased my interest to join. To understand more about LP4Y, I went to the Training and Development Center (TDC) Nepal which is located in Tinkune. After learning about the project I decided to utilize my free time by joining the 3-month professional life skill training of LP4Y. I joined the training in August 2022.

Green Village Nepal is a part of LP4Y project that aims to accompany young women towards professional integration by equipping them with life and soft skills. It is located in a green and rural area.

There were four micro-companies including Restaurant, Event Organizer, Digital Center and Sustainable Development, each with its own purpose. We had mock interviews to train ourselves to give interviews to the company of our choice. I was successfully hired by the Event Organization micro-company as an inventory officer. I started to work as an inventory officer with my different friends, who belonged to different backgrounds.

I was totally unaware about professional life before joining the GV. But later on, I got a chance to learn about the professional process of inventory management as well as learning about the huge differences between fake and real Job Market and the companies. Besides that, I found an environment where many Youths get chances to sharpen their skills through training. I was a shy person when presenting myself and to speak in front of people was one of my biggest fears but slowly it changed and I became able to organize awareness workshops among community people. While working with the team at GV, I learnt to find beauty in working with different people from different backgrounds. I was able to experience the power of unity, which has helped me a lot now as well.

Two months in Event micro-company was such an amazing experience. The last month of the training was based on job search, where we go door to door to find decent jobs by ourselves. It helps us to be Independent on what we want and how we want. I learnt to use Google Maps as an important tool of modern life.

While going door to door, I applied for a job at the Head Office of Labim Mall company and had an interview with the HR office of that company, while also doing an interview with Team Leader of Orchid company. Unfortunately, I failed to get a job in that company due to lack of citizenship (I am an orphan). I got many job opportunities but due to my lack of a citizenship card, I received no job offers. It made me feel down. I was losing all hopes towards life. Everything began blank: my confidence, my skills. I was suffering from anxiety and lost all my patience, even though I decided to talk about it with Coach. They found a partner named Kritan Adhikari who was a legal adviser.

After completing 3 months training (Entrepreneur step), I had a follow-up with Kirtan and people from the center where I live. Then, there was 7 months of follow-up to various government offices to fight for citizenship. Finally, while doing a search on the local places where I used to live before 15, I found my step father with the help of local people from the community and successfully made a citizenship card. Achieving a proof of nationality with a citizenship card was my biggest success ever in life. Forever I will be very grateful to every member of LP4Y project including Kirtan Adhikari and CPCS staff for unconditionally helping me to achieve my rights.

In 2022, I joined the STARS Club, which is an autonomous and a huge part of the LP4Y project. It's a group of those motivated Entrepreneurs who have successfully completed the 3-month Entrepreneur step. It's also a place where we can work from our own place. There are 6 important positions within the club and I am an Event Ambassador of the STARS Club. I organize events, workshops and maintain the processes of every step of the event. Workshops are my main responsibility. We have different responsibilities depending on our position in the Club and we work together to achieve together. *"Growing together to achieve more"* has become our main motto of the club.

Beside it, I am currently studying for a Bachelor second Year and working as an inventory officer at CPCS Organization. My work has become better now due to my team working experience from GV. I am working freely now and have basic rights as normal people. Imagine belonging to a country but lacking the basic proof of citizenship and being denied access to essential rights and opportunities due to the absence of a citizenship card. This creates the silent struggle for countless individuals. Therefore, I want to raise awareness about it and work with Youth such as myself. In the future, I want to write a story about my journey so that I can share a spark to those who have been feeling lost on their journey.

My journey taught me to find strengths in the darkest moment of my life where I had almost lost my hopes. I believe that everything happens for beautiful reasons in life. To those STARS who can shine brighter than they imagine, please let your dreams act as a compass to point you in the right direction, and your heart will light the way. *"YOU ARE CAPABLE FOR BRIGHTER DAYS."*

From Navotas to Bolloré: Dina's story

Dina Osabel - STARS - Aurora, The Philippines

I am Dina, a young woman who used to live in Navotas City. I used to live with my sister and brother only, because our father left us when I was 10 years old and our mother died due to a disease in 2016. When my mother died, my life turned upside down to the point that I attempted to end my own life because *"What is the point of doing everything now when my one and only motivation has gone?"*

But everything changed when the sister of my friend invited me to join Life Project 4 Youth. At first, I was following the training because I was bored at home. And as the time went by, I did not expect to feel as safe and accepted as I was in LP4Y. I was used to facing haters and judgmental people outside and trying to bring you down.

LP4Y became my home, a safe place where I can be myself and where the Catalysts will accompany us and help us to improve. Not only in the way we speak or write in English, but also how to use Microsoft, Excel and moreover how to be professional. One thing that I will never forget during my journey in LP4Y is that they made me realize that I can be a better version of myself.

I finished LP4Y during the pandemic. It was not easy, but I was hired as an admin assistant in one of the companies in Makati City. Unfortunately, it did not last long due to the pandemic. We had a skeletal schedule: no work, no pay. At that moment, I was living in Navotas. I was spending a lot of time in transportation, and it was expensive. I decided to end it.

I did extra work in my friend's small business while applying and sending resumés in as many companies as possible. I got interviews but no one accepted me because of my educational background. I was stuck in that routine for a year until one of the Coaches in LP4Y invited me to send my resume in Bolloré and do an interview. I grabbed that great opportunity, beginning my career as an International Freight Forwarding Operator in Bolloré.

First, I became an intern for 5 months in the Finance department. After that, they absorbed me as a custom compiler employee. Finally, after 6 months, I became a regular employee with a new job title as an International Freight Forwarding Operator. Bolloré helped me to improve myself and to develop my ability at work. Without the help of Bolloré and LP4Y together, I would have never been who I am and where I am now.

My advice to the Youth coming from extreme poverty: stop thinking that no one will accept your application because you do not have that ability and are not entitled since you are not a degree holder. Remember there are a lot of successful people without a college degree. And do not be afraid if you make a mistake because it is the sign that you are doing something.

A mistake does not mean that you are a failure. It is not how far you fall that is important but how high you bounce back to make a difference from your mistake.

Lost in life

Chaimaa Lagha - STARS - Green Village Lebanon

Before I joined the GV team, I was very lost in life. I lost my father when I was 13 years old and it really affected me. I struggled to live and it always felt like surviving. It got worse when I reached university. I no longer knew what I wanted. I changed my major twice in two years which made me lose a lot of time. It affected my mental health a lot because to live without a goal, a will, a dream and seeing your friends achieve their goals while you are still below zero hurts and breaks you inside rather than the frustrations you hear that you aren't good enough.

Then, my friend told me about LP4Y and the program. At the beginning, I hesitated and received some rejections from my surroundings. But two days before the starting of the program, I made the decision to join and to do something daring for myself for the first time, knowing that maybe this is an opportunity for me. I joined, not caring about anyone's opinion. I didn't know much about the program, I started my journey barely speaking English with a lot of strangers, an organized system, a new environment. Everything seemed scary to me at first, until I got to know the girls, the Coaches, understood how the system works which gave me more clarity in what I wanted.

In less than a month, I met 17 new people, became the first Youth leader which encouraged and motivated me further. I started working in the bank company as the finance and accounting officer, I started running my own business. I started valuing time, the responsibilities I had, I started to like having a day full with no wasted time. This was my second achievement, but I was still confused about my future. Whenever I was asked about what you want to become I had a different answer. The fact that I gave speeches and spoke in front of a lot of people made me realize that I want to work in media and become a social journalist united by people's voice. This became my passion and finally I entered the job search with full motivation. Yes, I can do it!

Finally, I thank the LP4Y team, the Catalysts, my friends and family and all the people who helped me in this big achievement in starting a new life.

Follow your dreams and trust the process

Tania Khalil & Zaynab Hammou - STARS - Green Village Lebanon

I'm Tania Khalil. I have a real passion in life: I love designing clothes. Alongside my studies, I spend a lot of time creating cool outfits at home. Looking back on my time at the Green Village, I'm thankful for all the lessons I learned there.
The Green Village taught me about being independent and trying new things, because becoming more independent also means taking responsibility for your dreams, following your passion and doing everything you can to achieve it.
Thanks to going there, I got to work at a cool fashion place last summer. It was a full-time job in summer where I had the opportunity to manage the fashion atelier. Unfortunately, I had to leave the job to continue my education but this experience made me even more determined to follow my dream to become a fashion designer. Indeed, it even gave me the idea of starting designing clothes at home! Taking old clothes and recycling them into beautiful designs: that is what I like to do now!

With hindsight, to other young people like me, I say: *"Keep going, even when things get tough. Finding the right job can be hard, but don't give up. Be brave, take chances, and remember that learning new things is always worth it."*

I'm Zeinab Hammoud. I work at CI College, and I'm studying French literature at the Lebanese University. Looking back on my time at the Green Village, I remember learning all the important things to reach the job market like being professional and managing my time well.

Navigating the job market in Lebanon, particularly as a woman, presents its unique challenges. However, my determination to become independent and demonstrate that women are capable of accomplishing anything they set their minds to remains unwavering. My journey to my current position wasn't straightforward. Initially, I explored opportunities through door-to-door inquiries, which led me to participate in a job fair alongside a group of inspiring individuals, referred to as STARS in LP4Y. It was during this fair, and with a renewed application to CI College, that I successfully secured my role in administration.

My advice to those who dare to dream big is simple: never give up. Stepping out of your comfort zone, building new connections, and embracing continuous learning are crucial steps towards realizing your ambitions. The path may seem daunting at times, but with collective support and a steadfast belief in your capabilities, success is within our reach.

The most important thing I learned is to dream

Babita Baniya - Entrepreneur - Kathmandu, Nepal

Namaste! My name is Babita Baniya. I live in Shantinagar. I am 21 years old. I joined LP4Y in February 2021. Now, I am in the Entrepreneur step. Currently, I am working on my own.

Before coming to LP4Y I worked as a housemaid for two months. But it was really difficult to satisfy them and also I had to work a lot and I was paid very little so I left it. Then, I worked as a laborer in the construction of new houses. I worked as a laborer until I was 8 months pregnant. I earned a good amount while I was working there and I managed to save 2 Lakhs ($1,680). But my husband got sick and had to spend that money on his operation. After that, I had a baby boy and I was not doing anything at home so my landlady told me about LP4Y. I came to the center with her and I liked the program of LP4Y and I joined it.

In LP4Y, I learned many things. First day of joining LP4Y, there was computer training. I had never seen a computer in my life. When I touched it, I was so scared. I was thinking if I didn't touch it in the right way, I might damage the computer. My friends and Coaches taught me how to operate the computer. After that I could type, use Gmail, make a budget sheet, etc. I also learned English. Before coming to LP4Y I didn't even know how to speak Nepali well because I come from a really remote place in Nepal where they speak Nepali in a different way. I never went to school, but after coming to LP4Y I learned to read and write both in Nepali and English as I had to learn it to do the training. I took some time at home and learnt it with the help of a sister who was living near to my place. In the center I tried to speak with my friends and Coaches and I improved a lot. I also learned how to communicate with people well.

During the lockdown, my husband didn't have any work, we didn't have any money left, our gas cylinder was empty and we were not able to pay the house rent. I was so worried. At the same time, the sister living near to my room approached me and said let's sell some vegetables together. So, we went to the market place to see how it works.

It was the season of maize so I thought of bringing maize and selling it door to door. First time I bought maize for NRS.500 ($4.20) and carried it in a basket made of Himalayan Bamboo. I went door to door, I was feeling a little bit awkward and shy but in my mind I was thinking that I have to sell it to get my money back and I managed to sell all of it and came back with NRS. 600 ($5.04) profit. There are 3 sizes of maize I buy with different prices: small size NRS. 4/pc, medium size NRS. 7/pc and large size NRS.10/pc, and I sell it at double price. I carry it in a doko (basket) and sell it near my area and the Baneshwor area. If I buy the maize for NRS. 700-800 ($5.88-$6.77), I get a profit of NRS. 1500-1600 ($12.06-$13.44) if I sell everything. On Sunday, Monday and Tuesday people fast in Nepal, so I sell more and earn more profit. In these three days if I sell the maize for NRS.

900-1000 ($7.56-$8.40), I get a profit of NRS. 2,000-3,000 ($16.80-$25.21). Because when they fast, they can still eat maize and different kinds of spinach which are considered pure.

I use the earned money on the household goods, pay the rent and for baby care products. I save and deposit the rest of the money in my bank account as well as my son's account. My dream job is to open a small shop, so with the saved money I plan to open a small meat and vegetable shop with my husband, because I have experience and knowledge on selling vegetables. I use my savings for my son's education and emergency healthcare. I am really satisfied with the work I am doing now because if you work in another place other control you and you earn less. Now, I am working on my own and I am the boss. I earn around NRS. 35,000-40,000 ($290-$340) per month.

I learned many things after coming to LP4Y. The most important thing I learned is to dream because I never thought that we could dream and reach that. I learned to be independent, learnt how to communicate with the customer effectively, and how to communicate with known and unknown people. I use this skill in the work I am doing now. I can stand on my own feet and feed my family. I am independent now.

I want to advise the Youth who are in LP4Y that there are enough opportunities if you search. You need to accept whatever jobs you get to gain some experience. We should not be lazy and sit still. Everything is difficult in the beginning but if you start working on it, you will reach success. We must be independent and should have courage to stand on our own feet.

I want to thank all the Coaches of LP4Y. I learned many things in LP4Y. I learned to be independent and be strong. Thank you Coaches and thank you all.

CHAPTER REFLECTION

How does your vision for the future reflect your core values?

Think of ways that your ambitions align with what you believe in.

CHAPTER 3: COMMUNITY & SOLIDARITY

No journey is undertaken alone and the strength of community plays a crucial role in shaping our paths. This chapter highlights the profound impact of community and solidarity in the lives of Youth. Through compelling narratives, we will explore how coming together as a unified force fosters support, encouragement and collective growth. The stories of community-based initiatives will illustrate the transformative power of solidarity in overcoming challenges and achieving common goals. This chapter serves as a reminder that, together, we are stronger and that the bonds of community can drive meaningful change.

From the Slums to the United Nations
Alexia Gaube - Catalyst - New York, USA

What would you do if you were 18, living in a slum or on the street, out of school because you couldn't afford it, and forced to pick through trash to survive? What if you had no money, no legal identity, and already one or two children? What if you were systematically rejected by society because of where you live and what it represents to others?

These questions rarely crossed my mind when I was young. I am one of the fortunate people on this planet who had a childhood with support, a roof over my head, food, a safe environment and access to education. I had the privilege of choosing my professional path. Although I saw poverty, I never truly grasped its full implications, probably because I couldn't imagine myself in that context.

My perspective began to shift when I traveled to South America for my studies and met Youth living in these circumstances. They shared their truths and concerns, things I had never experienced. Leaving them, I felt a mix of gratitude and guilt. These young people could have been me or my relatives under different circumstances. So, "Why me?" Why did I have opportunities that they didn't? These young people had passions, dreams and skills. They wanted to make their families proud and find their place in the world. The only difference was that they weren't born into favorable conditions.
Seeing their creativity, dedication, ingenuity, resourcefulness, and eagerness, it was clear they

deserved so much more than what life had given them. They deserved so much more to be in my shoes.

As I embraced this reality, I decided to fight against this injustice and find a way to help people get the opportunities they deserve. This commitment began in my own country alongside my corporate job and eventually led me to work in Indian and Filipino slums with LP4Y. This experience profoundly impacted me.

When I first considered international solidarity work, many causes caught my attention, but one stood out: LP4Y. LP4Y offers a concrete, sustainable solution to empower young people while also supporting local communities. LP4Y is not just another charity; we don't use that word because we don't do charity. Instead, we empower Youth to achieve the better life they deserve. We help them reveal their talents, stand up for themselves, support their families and ultimately escape poverty.

LP4Y's unique pedagogy efficiently provides the tools and confidence these young people need to enter the decent world they once saw as a distant dream. Our comprehensive inclusion method creates a local movement for inclusion. Over a few months, participants grow both personally and professionally. They develop skills and gain awareness of physical and mental well-being, citizenship and rights, and environmental and climate issues. They become active change leaders for themselves and their communities, serving as role models for other Youth who have lost hope.

The LP4Y experience began by stepping into the unknown, leaving behind my comfortable life to live frugally in the slums alongside the other Catalysts on this journey. This proximity to the Youth is essential to the model, allowing us to understand their reality as much as possible and ensuring that all funds are efficiently invested directly into the Youth programs.

Drawing on my corporate background, I started as the Coordinator of the Youth Inclusion Network (YIN), a network of companies committed to the inclusion of Youth from excluded backgrounds, initiated by LP4Y. Together, we implemented professional inclusion initiatives and facilitated the sharing of best practices. This enriching experience, connecting slums to business districts, brings about successful outcomes and life-changing opportunities for both young people and employees. Employees who met these Youth came to understand their potential and became advocates for inclusion. These young people possess the extraordinary ability to break down barriers when given the opportunity to be heard.

My second experience with LP4Y was as a Coach in Cebu, The Philippines, where I accompanied the Youth through a six-month training program. Working with them and assisting in their development was an incredibly enriching experience. There are many anecdotes I could share, but I'd like to highlight one aspect that LP4Y excels in and is my favorite part of being a Coach: "the call."

This moment represents when the Youth, initially shy and fearful of making mistakes and facing rejection again, begin to take initiative and dare to accept responsibilities. At the start, they don't understand why we, the Catalysts and other Youth, believe in them - something they've rarely experienced. But gradually, through training, work sessions, and conversations, we see them transform. I vividly remember Judy, who had been very quiet, suddenly standing up during our morning check-in and saying, "Me coach, I will do the team briefing". She volunteered to lead the task of outlining the day's work activities in front of all the Youth, stepping completely out of her comfort zone. From that moment, her progress was spectacular. This pivotal moment not only boosts their confidence but also empowers the entire team, fostering peer encouragement and community advocacy. It instills sustainable motivation, inclusion, and active Youth engagement, enabling them to lead change initiatives for themselves, their families, and other excluded Youth. Some of them have even joined LP4Y as colleagues after achieving professional success, paying it forward by guiding others through their empowerment journey.

Coaching is not easy, but it has given me an in-depth understanding of some of the most inspiring young people - resilient, committed individuals full of potential, creativity, talents, and generosity despite facing critical situations. Accompanying them is challenging, but each day brings a new victory.

Take Kathy, for example. She learned what a decent job is and refused an offer because she understood she deserved to live with dignity. She is now a proud administrative assistant. Then there's Peter, who I briefly coached in our jail program. Despite spending five years in jail as an innocent man, he found hope again to fight for his case and future. He now works for a large construction company.

Eric, who endured some of the hardest stories I've ever heard, discovered his talents and now works in finance at a big hotel, paying for his sister's college education. Marta, abandoned by her family at birth and the most dedicated person I've met, had a child at 15 and couldn't continue school. She now proudly works in a restaurant and can afford medical support for her sick daughter.

I also came to New York City as LP4Y's Main Representative to the United Nations. Since 2020, LP4Y has held Special Consultative Status at the United Nations Economic and Social Council (ECOSOC). This status recognizes LP4Y as an expert and representative of civil society at the UN, tasked with amplifying the voices of young people experiencing extreme poverty and exclusion. My ultimate goal here is to spread their stories to the world, but I am not doing this alone. With me are the narratives of the young people and whenever possible them in person, along with the determination to give them the platform they need to voice their challenges and needs.

Benefiting from technical and unique grassroots expertise in multiple countries, LP4Y actively campaigns within UN committees and commissions in NYC and worldwide. Today, LP4Y is considered the Youth inclusion expert of the NGO Committee for

Social Development, and our expertise is sought by other organizations and UN entities.

We raise the alarm on the current situation in slums and highlight the crucial importance and power of involving excluded Youth. We share practical, multilateral solutions to promote partnerships and a culture of accountability, linking statements with concrete, meaningful, and effective actions. We deliver oral and written statements, organize and participate in events and expert panels, meet with member states, and support working coalitions for Youth inclusion and young women. Most importantly, LP4Y provides vulnerable Youth with opportunities to share their realities and perspectives with UN officials and member state representatives, ensuring their voices are finally heard by institutions and policymakers.

At the UN, our role as an international movement is crucial: we illustrate challenges and propose concrete solutions to influence local decisions towards greater equity and more tailored solutions to grassroots issues. Vulnerable young people are essential to this mission; they are our experts. They possess solutions and practical insights for community issues. Consulting them is the only way to identify overlooked barriers and reveal tangible solutions that bridge the gap between the intended and actual outcomes of policies. They have the potential to create profound global and local impacts, harnessing the energy to implement and monitor actions within their communities and local governments.

Impacting policy-making is a long-term endeavor that contrasts with the rapid achievements of the Youth in the field. However, when young people finally get the chance to speak directly to UN officials and express their views, the difference is immediate and profound. Each intervention creates a lasting impact, accelerating the urgency to remove barriers to the inclusive participation of vulnerable Youth. These young people become ambassadors of solutions for a better future, from the slums to the United Nations.

Their unique perspectives and experiences challenge conventional viewpoints, transforming impersonal reports into personal stories. Numbers become names of individuals affected by the challenges outlined in the UN's 17 Sustainable Development Goals. Their messages resonate, reminding representatives of their duties and reinforcing their accountability in supporting civil society's access to more rights and opportunities for their entire communities.

Building speeches with the Youth and watching them shine as they take the microphone is my favorite part of this mission. Initially, they don't realize how incredible their stories are, how strong and impactful they are, and how their lives, which they consider ordinary, exemplify commitment to meaningful change in their communities. They are the embodiment of resilience, capable of far more than they imagine.

As we work together to identify the key elements and messages they want to share, I learn from their visions of life, dreams, little victories, and achievements—the most inspiring lessons imaginable. They are a humbling testament to humanity. Each testimony brings a new thrill, a new story, a new emotion. Supporting these young people overwhelms me as much as it strengthens my resolve to push forward.

For instance, when Laxmi, a young woman from India who was excluded by her traditional society for wanting to be free, suddenly improvised a full speech on women's empowerment and independence in front of a major corporation in the US. Or when Dian explained to the UN the need to change their language to make it more accessible and encourage contributions from vulnerable people. Or when Soumayraa declared during an official UN ceremony, "*I want women to enter society and obtain all their rights.*"

These moments are not just inspirational; they are powerful calls to action, showcasing the incredible potential of these young people to drive change on both a local and global scale.

Beyond the pride visible in their eyes as they speak—an achievement that surpasses all expectations—these young people become the voices and symbols of the hundreds of millions of Youths around the world who are seldom heard. Their access to such platforms would have been nearly impossible without the unwavering support of LP4Y contributors worldwide and the hard work of Catalysts and partners in the field who help them recognize their potential.

These incredible Youths, who previously lacked opportunities and were forced into paths they did not choose, have finally found their conviction. Thanks to their newfound skills and confidence, they now embrace powerful roles, gain recognition, and pursue futures they once thought unattainable. This transformation would not be possible without our collective commitment.
There are countless ways to support Youth: by accompanying them, backing the organizations that empower them, trusting the potential of those without traditional resumes but with a willingness to learn, and changing how we perceive others' abilities to contribute. It is our responsibility to make the world a better place, to break biases, and to ensure that every young person can embrace their chosen path without being limited by their background.

Together, let's make a difference - for the Youth, their children, their communities, and for humanity. As Sherlyn Caasi, a Program Alumni who became a Coach and remains a profound source of inspiration for me, said in her UN speech: "*These changes depend on you. You've heard our voices - now let's see your actions!*"

Losing my passport in the Philippines, Oh my God!

Albertine Corne - Country Coordinator, Indonesia

This is the story of the day I lost my passport in Manila, or an ode to the power of community.

It's early 2023. Some countries require a third dose of the Covid-19 vaccine to travel freely. Unfortunately, I'm allergic to iodine and the doctors only recommend the Pfizer vaccine, which is of course unavailable in my mission country, Indonesia.

I take advantage of the Welcome Weeks in the Philippines to find out more: it's available here! A week before my return to Indonesia, I take all the necessary documents and walk up the street from Taguig to the hospital. The street vendors shout to drown out the noise of tricycles and children playing basketball. I pass some of the neighbors I've become accustomed to greeting over the past 2 weeks.

When I arrive at the hospital, I'm quickly taken care of and vaccinated without being asked too many questions. I return home the same way. A good thing done.

What a surprise two days later! While checking my belongings for my departure, I discover that my passport is missing. I searched the room from top to bottom. It must be there; I used it at the hospital two days earlier! But after a frantic search, I have to face the facts: my passport isn't in the apartment. My housemates, worried about me, empty their cupboards and comb the whole center. It definitely fell out of my bag on the 400-meter walk to the hospital.

The first reflexes quickly kicked in: call the embassy, which tells me I will be stuck in the Philippines for 45 days while the document is being redone, and that I will have to pay a fee because my visa was about to expire. I warn the teams in Indonesia that I will not be coming back straight away, and that I will have to coordinate things remotely. Then I check whether the plane tickets are exchangeable. Losing one's passport is the fear of anyone living abroad.

I slowly recover from the emotions of the day and sit down on the sofa in the Catalyst area of the center. Lucie Dubert's book *"Bahini"* is on the coffee table. I read it a few months ago. Suddenly, a passage comes to my mind. She had lost her passport a few days before leaving Nepal, and a community vendor had helped her find it. If Lucie can do it, so can I! I grab my phone and some money and tell everyone I'm not going home tonight without my passport.

The first step is to go and see the Youth, who are preparing to debrief for the day. I explain my situation to them, and they assure me that they'll talk to everyone around them to find out if anyone has seen it. They feel sorry for me and the *"good luck Coach"* sounds pessimistic.

Then, I call out to the group of children who play in front of the center every day. We're going on a treasure hunt! *"The first to find the passport wins a huge packet of sweets."* Excitement is running high! They start running around, bringing me objects and asking me with hopeful eyes: *"This?"* After 20 minutes, fatigue and exasperation have won out over the game. I say goodbye and thank you for the joy.

I start walking up the whole street to the hospital. It's not that big, it's got to be somewhere. My goal is to stop at every store on the street. No exceptions. Obviously, no one has seen my passport, but everyone seems concerned. I'm advised to go and see the garbage collection service, who have probably been there the previous two days. I take a tricycle to get there. Behind their bulbous garbage cans, the garbage collectors give me a negative nod. One of them redirects me to Baranguay, the local municipality.

Arriving at Baranguay, I'm asked to make a statement at the police station, before being allowed to enter the Baranguay mayor's office. He suggests I make an announcement that will be broadcasted over all the street microphones. It's late, I've been searching for 3 hours, and I cling to this last hope, telling myself I'll go home afterwards empty-handed. The mayor ushers me into the technical room. Dozens of screens are on the walls. The entire neighborhood is under surveillance. I'm impressed, but mostly surprised! He turns on his microphone and starts shouting his message in Tagalog.

I thank him warmly and head downstairs. On the stairs, a stranger grabs my arm and starts shouting to her colleagues. *"You are the passport woman?"* Yes, that's me. Hope returns, it's been found!

The neighbor of a local shopkeeper whom I'd interviewed a few hours earlier had found it on the ground the day before. This evening, she had learned that a stranger was scouring the neighborhood for it. She had posted the photo of the passport on all her friends' groups, calling on anyone who had come across me to contact her. We had been searching for each other for 3 hours.

Happily, she gives it back to me along with a hug and a little push. She tells me to be careful, and we end the evening with a group photo with all the members of the Taguig Barangay.

It's a great lesson for me: always believe in the power of community in excluded areas! (And to be more careful with my documents).

All the Youth, STARS and Catalysts to support Tondo!

Mariechu Peralta - Catalyst - Tondo, The Philippines

I am Mariechu Peralta, previously of the program Bloom here in LPC Tondo. I am currently working for LP4Y as a Coach for the Entrepreneurs, after becoming myself a Catalyst. I am helping them to find a decent job, and also trying to motivate them to fulfill all their dreams.

I am leading the STARS Club, which is a group of Youth who finished the PTE (the Professional Training for Entrepreneurs in LP4Y) and now have to face the real world, outside Life Project Centers. I am here to accompany them because I know that we can suddenly feel stressed when we don't find a job. This is never easy but the key is to never give up!

Last April 18th, it was around 7am in the morning and 50% of the people in Happyland were still sleeping, when they woke-up in panic because a fire started to grow. We were all shocked. The damages of the fire affected around 500 houses and families. I was also sleeping in my house in Happyland when the fire started. Fortunately, even though I was affected, the fire didn't hit my house totally. I am lucky. But I was so afraid for the other STARS and Youth of LP4Y who were in the middle of the fire... They were already facing the Covid-19 pandemic, a really hard time for us.

I immediately tried to think of how I could help and started to reach some STARS. It was wonderful to see that all of them participated to give food packs and clothes for those who were the most impacted. Expats in Manila organized some collections as well.

I am thankful for my colleagues who helped me, especially Anariza Cajodo and Axelle, who take care of the kids at the Little Angels Academy in

Tondo, as they are the ones who collected the relief goods from the community.

I saw that even if we are facing a crisis, these people around me still wanted to help the most in need. Even the Youth affected by the fire contributed to distribute the donations collected by LP4Y, expats and community. At this moment, I felt like I understood what the motto of LP4Y *"Together We Can" really means*. LP4Y created a special fire crisis fund, it helped a lot of STARS and Youth to re-build their houses. So thank you to all the donors for giving donations to LP4Y. This is helping a lot of our community to stay strong facing new crises. We will for sure continue to mobilize and help the community.

And finally I am so thankful to all the volunteers who are still motivated to help the Youth even during the pandemic.

Collect experiences and create your worth

Ian Buenavis - STARS President - Payatas, The Philippines

My name is Ian Buenavista, a motivated 21 years old man from Manila, The Philippines. I joined LP4Y in the year 2016. Before joining LP4Y, I used to live in the province. I just graduated from high school and got a scholarship from the university. However, in an unfortunate time, my father died and we got into a serious financial problem. That is why I stopped studying and from a young age I learned to be independent and work in the wet market where I tried different work. I can say that I never had a purpose in life.

God's timing is so perfect that he let me meet LP4Y. It may not be the timing and the things I want, but it's the timing I need in life. My relatives far from the province asked me to consider LP4Y. I came here to Manila living in my aunt's house to learn more about LP4Y. When I heard about it, the word *"Scam"* was the first thing that came to my mind but then I gave it a try and considered it. I remember myself saying *"If I don't try then I will never know"*. Since I am a Youth with a lot of curiosity, I started to go to the center. Step by step, I learned a lot from a starting point of being shy, not confident, not good in English, from being a Youth who doesn't know computer skills and who comes from the countryside.

The Coaches patiently and consistently taught me the things I needed to learn. It started from the process of micro-company and how the business works on-hand. I have learned to be a responsible Youth, not only to myself but also to the people around me. What I learned in LP4Y has been my armor to fight for my position in life. LP4Y helped me build and improve my qualities and skills that are very helpful because all the things I did in LP4Y are the same things inside the company from inventory, processing of records and files and being a great team player.

LP4Y really is a foundation for experience: Time management for being punctual; being responsible; being a leader; focusing more on the objective; and different skills like communication skills, English, email and computer skills; and being a professional worker while helping the company towards its growth. Most importantly, I learned to be a role model for the other Youth.

I am also proud and happy to be the President of Quezon City LP4Y STARS Club who's still assisting the Youth in the center by providing training and building the communication link between the STARS who graduated in LP4Y and the Youth currently in the program.

I started in CGI as a Global HR Member Services Associate and worked with my team for 2 years. The opportunity of working in a Global IT company such as CGI makes me very grateful, but then of course it is a challenging environment and I have been criticized due to the lack of documentation or degree. In these challenging times, I have realized and proved that LP4Y Youth are the most equipped Youth with skills needed in every position in every company.

After 2 years in HR, I grabbed the opportunity to move to the Financial Shared Services as a Payroll Junior Consultant in CGI and I am still working hard and doing what I have to do for my personal growth, the growth of the company and the people around me. I am currently working at home with the privilege given by the CGI and now I can focus more on my own improvement as I am currently studying in Polytechnic University of the Philippines, taking up Business of Arts in Broadcasting and have time for the Quezon City STARS Club improvement. I realized all this time that we don't have to be great to start, but we have to start to be great. To focus on the positive and learn a lot from the experiences because your simple experiences and your stories could help someone else to be motivated in life!

Last February from the 2nd to the 6th, I was given an opportunity to become an Assistant Coach and be a volunteer for one week in Payatas Quezon City, Manila for the PayataSport Team. I had a great week with the Youth and I have seen their professionalism and responsibility skills during my stay. While helping them learn, I, myself, learned from them too and can see the team spirit with one dream to succeed in the future. From this experience, I learned to appreciate life even if it's not perfect and was reminded that happiness is not a fulfillment of what we wish for, but an appreciation of what we have and what we can provide. I am very thankful and grateful for this opportunity that I will cherish my whole life.

From Witness to Advocate: How LP4Y Transforms Lives

Chloe Sebag - LP4Y Partner - New York, USA

When I first heard about LP4Y, it was from one of its NYC representatives at the time. They needed volunteers for a gala and when I heard about its mission and actions, I already thought what they did was amazing. Amazing because it gave another chance at life for those who have been misfortuned and were born somewhere where girls are made to marry, and boys are meant to provide. A world where getting paid less than a dollar a day becomes the norm. I had never before seen an NGO that is focused in the way that LP4Y is, on young adults. Early adult years (18-25), are some of, if not the most important years for a person to forge their place in society. And LP4Y helps Youth to do exactly that.

What impressed me and also attracted me to LP4Y was the Catalyst's continuous involvement in the Youth's lives, and LP4Y's everlasting ecosystem. Not only do they make sure they get a job once they leave the program, but they make sure the Youth are equipped to get jobs, and to keep their jobs for the rest of their lives.

I've heard about it from others and I've seen it firsthand. In the summer of 2022, I was
in India, where I spent some time with the Youth accompanied by LP4Y. We went to visit a former Youth at her job. LP4Y encourages the young adults to come up with a Life Project Plan which is their dream ambition. Hers was to become a nurse. At this time, she couldn't yet be, as this career requires many degrees and years at university, so currently she was a secretary at a medical office. An office that was climatized, where the employees wore uniforms and all had a smile on their face that we could just feel, was genuine. As we walked into the center of the room, her eyes lit up. "Romain, Carla!

Oh I am so happy to see you!" ...as she hugged them both.

Romain and Carla both had accompanied her in her journey with LP4Y, for day to day activities and events, they supported her. But, what they also did - which I think is what helps the Youth most - was let her figure things out herself. LP4Y has a very particular approach. For instance, when Youth don't know a word of English, instead of a local Coach translating it from their native language, they were encouraged to describe it, in words that they did know. And whether it be a word that she doesn't know how to say in English, a plumbing problem or a personal situation, what the Youth are taught is not what to do, but how to do it. This is because LP4Y focuses on giving Youth the tools to succeed, and not putting them in front of its doors, which is also the reason why it works so well.

From going door-to-door in Katmandu's slums to "recruit" Youth to seeing them at STARS events, the difference was immense. After only 3 or 6 months, many could speak English proficiently, utilize computers and technology, were better leaders, and overall commanded better conversations and interactions. In the short span of three months (at Green Villages), the Youth had made tremendous progress in so many different areas and seeing the difference in between Youth in their first week at the GV and one in their last one really helps understand the impact that LP4Y has.

Being at the centers to see this in real life was the best experience I could ever hope for, but sadly, not everyone can take the time to do what I did. So, what can we do at our scales, from the U.S, or France or any other place for that matter? We can advocate. We can share our stories, share the Youth's stories, statistics, emotion and so much more.

There are many ways by which you can get involved in LP4Y and advocacy, as it is one of the three pillars of the movement (advocate, encourage and accompany), is not less important than funding it or accompanying youth day to day. So, I encourage you, wherever you are, whoever you are and whatever you do, to take action to support LP4Y, so it can keep pulling deserving young adults out of poverty's vicious circle.

A Coaching Journey of Gratitude

Sandra Halabi - Former Coach - Beirut, Lebanon

I still vividly remember my first visit to the Training and Development Center of Bourj Hammoud.
The narrow streets, the warm and welcoming greetings of the shopkeepers made me feel as if I had known them forever. When I stepped into the Training and Development Center in Beirut, I had a deep sense that this was the first visit of many.
My arrival coincided with the C4C program, where I witnessed over 40 small children receiving training from inspiring young women. Their responsibility and multitasking abilities left a lasting impression. As my days passed during my Coaching mission with LP4Y, my initial impression was confirmed.

One of the things I admired in my mission is the home visits which usually give us a chance to see the environment in which the Youth are living. I was always amazed by the kind-hearted parents who spoke warmly about LP4Y and their gratitude for the opportunities it provided to their children. Their stories, such as the one I will share below, never fail to make an impact (on my personal life).

Upon entering the home of Sidra, a Youth at TDC Beirut, I was warmly greeted by her mother who embraced me, making me feel like her own daughter, despite it being our first meeting. As I prepared to sit with Sidra's family on a small carpet, a little girl, not more than 5 years old, ran over and hugged me tightly, providing a beautiful interruption filled with love.

The mother expressed her gratitude for the opportunities her daughter had received through LP4Y. However, her focus remained on her children and the hardships they endured, having fled from war-torn Syria to Lebanon. I was deeply moved, listening to her story and empathizing with her experiences, amazed by her resilience. In response, I asked a simple yet profound question: "*And you Fattoum (her name), how do you feel?*" With a small, heartfelt smile and tears in her eyes, she looked at me and said, "*I am good now. Do you know what my dream is?*" Her response caught me by surprise, and I felt a mix of emotions as I inquired further about her dream. She answered without hesitation, "*My dream is to find someone who can write down my life story because I am illiterate, and I believe that what I have lived deserves to be shared. It's like a movie!*" Her words left me both curious about her story and apprehensive about what I might hear.

I may not possess the writing skills to effectively convey to readers all the information that Fattoum shared with me. However, if you happen to know a proficient writer or someone talented in crafting documentaries, I am more than willing to facilitate the connection between Fattoum and that person.

I wish I could articulate my emotions more precisely, but all I can say is that I deeply appreciate this opportunity to share this story with you and, maybe, play a part in making Fattoum's dream reality. I did not expect better than this ending to wrap up my Coaching journey in LP4Y which was absolutely full of gratitude and inspiration!

Making the world a better place

Carlos Walter - Biomedical Engineer - General Electric

Hi all! I'm Carlos Walter, a Mexican Biomedical Engineer doing a Leadership program in General Electric Healthcare. You probably wonder what my story is doing here. I do so too.

A couple of months after I joined GE, I was invited to

a call where they needed volunteers for a project that was changing the world for a lot of people. I decided to join to understand what they meant by "*changing the world*" and how I could contribute. As soon as they started, they introduced LP4Y, how they operate, what they do, and how they are, with no question, changing the world. I immediately wanted to be in, I wanted to be a part of such an amazing project. I wanted to help change the world.

The way I did that was by creating educational content for the Youth centers, along with a great group of volunteers from all over the world, connected by one thing; we were all employees of General Electric who wanted to collaborate with LP4Y. I started creating one small introduction to public speaking and storytelling, which is, at least in my opinion, one of the most important skills that needed to be developed. Once I got started, I realized a brief introduction was not going to be enough, so I decided to create more sessions for the topic. The result was a five-session program with different topics, all related to the selected skills. The rest of the volunteers also created amazing programs for different skills, like how to create a CV, Excel skills, brand management, among others.

The content that we created was going to be used with the instructors in centers welcoming the Youth. Unfortunately, though, this moment coincided with a new global crisis that reshaped everything we used to know; the pandemic known as COVID-19. Because of this, LP4Y, along with the team that coordinated GE volunteers, had to work fast to try to adapt to these new conditions. I was lucky enough to be invited to be part of the amazing team that works directly with LP4Y and coordinates volunteers from GE, a small team of real-life heroes within the company that calls themselves "*Youthful team.*"

We started working on switching the content we had created, as well as some other content created by the incredible pedagogy team from LP4Y, into digital programs that can be accessed anywhere with an internet connection. More volunteers joined the cause, and they are currently working hard to create the programs on the digital platform and creating new content for the Youth.

It has been an amazing opportunity, and I am grateful every day, both for being able to volunteer for the Youthful Team and the LP4Y organization. I can say, with no question, that this whole experience and collaboration has changed my world for the better.

One thing we know for sure is that, by doing these small actions, and having the courses on a digital platform, we are becoming participants of the actions that are making the

world a better place, with the Youth team and LP4Y leading the change.

Collaboration Story: LP4Y Nepal & Project Uddeshya

Suraj Silwal - Founder - Project Uddeshya - Nepal

Project Uddeshya is a young initiative born during the hard times of the COVID-19 outbreak when people were distressed inside their homes.

Project Uddeshya started as an online platform to talk about mental health. We organized online counseling sessions targeting students in a small village in rural Chitwan (South Nepal), and slowly marched toward sensitive issues relating to mental health with hundreds of students who were preparing for admissions for highschool and universities.

We envisioned an idea of designing art-based workshops which would promote emotional and mental wellbeing among communities. Finally, as the lockdown loosened, art-integrated mental wellbeing and physical training was implemented. This would be the stepping stone for a long-term partnership between Project Uddeshya and LP4Y. It was by chance that LP4Y and Project Uddeshya learned about one another and in October 2021,

Project Uddeshya formally reached out to LP4Y to expand its work portfolio.

We explained our work and organized trial workshops wearing masks as COVID-19 was still not over. With every session we organized, LP4Y and Project Uddeshya have come closer.

We have been fortunate to conduct numerous workshops on various topics, including music, theater, art, photography, jewelry making, incense making, legal counseling, nutrition consultation, health checkups, dignified menstruation, films, and mental counseling services that have helped Youths while honing our team to a new level. These workshops have been supported by several other Youth volunteers globally who are passionate about giving back to the community.

LP4Y has provided us with a platform to expand our volunteer initiative, build networks, and grow our work. It's also supported with the identification and collaboration of many Youth volunteers who want to give back to our community while expanding their network. We have partnered with multiple national and international organizations and recently our wellbeing workshops which we designed for Youth in LP4Y have been recognized by UNESCO as well as the British Council.

It's been almost 3 years now and we are still working together with LP4Y, and it brings us immense pleasure to witness the impactful work LP4Y is doing. Their openness to connect and collaborate with other Youth like us within the community means a lot!

Working as a Team Leader with 3 LP4Y Graduates

Ian Reoperez - LP4Y Partner - Decathlon, The Philippines

LP4Y has been our most successful partner in finding talented and passionate young teammates who can be contributors in our mission of making sports accessible to all. I had the pleasure of working with and leading several teammates over the years here in the company and today they are big contributors to the stores that they are a part of.

Currently in Decathlon Pasay, we have 3 Teammates who were a part of LP4Y. The most experienced one is a Sport Leader managing an important sport department in our store and also a Captain of the Day (a big responsibility in our organization) while another teammate is someone who transferred from Alabang and is a specialist in our Cashing Up processes and customer service. Our newest teammate, Wendy, is someone we met just last November, and we are pleased with the level of professionalism and enthusiasm she is showing with us in her first few months.

Overall, I find the Youth from LP4Y to be very hard-working teammates, always giving their best, always positive, and very optimistic to the challenges we face. They always seize the opportunity presented to them, and it has been a pleasure to see some of them show significant growth over the last few years. This is a partnership we wish to continue, and we are hoping to find even more talents in the future coming from LP4Y!

One month to dive into the Green Village pedagogy in Nepal

Elise Descamps - Volunteer – USA

Distributing pre-ordered croissants to neighbors in the morning; participating in the remarkable LP4Y Galas in New York; joining in the famous White Parties; promoting the Together We Art partnership with artists; holding high-school wide assemblies with LP4Y founders and Coaches were amongst the activities that the LP4Y Club at the French American School of New York was involved in. This is how I first engaged with LP4Y.

LP4Y USA leverages all those that care and who want to join the LP4Y movement, and from the youngest age, high-school students are encouraged to participate in fundraising and awareness activities, either alongside parents or through their own initiative. I was already actively committed to the LP4Y movement in High School, and had remained in touch. Then four years after graduating I had the amazing good fortune to visit the LP4Y Green Village in Godawari, Nepal. My immersion in the GV pedagogy surpassed all my previous experiences with LP4Y. Here's what truly stood out.

The learning-by-doing approach in action

First, what really stood out to me was to see the LP4Y learning-by-doing approach in action. Mornings start with a professional handshake in company uniform, an energizer, a public announcement of the news, a roundtable of the daily tasks by micro-companies, a discussion on business mantras, and then the Youth split into their micro-company teams, ready for a day of work. The Green Village is home to 4 micro-companies: Restaurant, Digital Center, Events, and Sustainable Development, each consisting of different positions (HR, Finance officer, communication officer, team leader…)

One event that really touched me was the graduation event. On top of being a truly inspiring moment, it is also one that perfectly encapsulates how the micro-companies work together in the LP4Y learning-by-doing approach:

"For a graduation event happening every month, Event Micro-Company team members will prepare speeches in English, will order beverages from the Restaurant company, will ask the Digital Center to print certificates and buy frames… Of

course, everything needs to be billed, quotations are to be made, professional invitations and emails are sent, and everything is to be photographed and reported in weekly reports, newsletters, social media accounts, and business presentations."

I was so impressed to see to what extent the girls do everything by themselves, working as a team to reach that common goal and distributing tasks. This is just a single joyful example, but alongside mock interviews conducted by partners, weekly guidance sessions with Coaches, handovers of positions, English classes, and all the tasks that need to be fulfilled in each micro-company, these women truly learn how to work with each other, build public-speaking skills, promote their confidence, and learn how the business world works, all in a practical way. This all makes the Youth ready to autonomously find jobs and succeed in their positions.

The strength of the LP4Y ecosystem

Second, all of this would not be possible without the entire LP4Y ecosystem. This ranges from HR to the brilliant Coaches they recruit, including the pedagogy team that guides Coaches, the partnership team, the leaders, the local partners, ... and the list goes on.

Each person implicated in the project has a specific role that makes them excel at it, and this is reflected in the rapid development of the Youth. It was truly admirable and inspiring to see such passion at all levels of the ecosystem, whether it be internally, in partnerships locally and globally, where everyone is so determined in fighting for Youth inclusion together.

Indonesia's food: How to survive with local community

Mathieu Navet - Coach - Jakarta, Indonesia

"You have been selected for a Coach position in TDC Jakarta, starting in February 2023." That's how it started. At the time, I had no idea what I was about to experience. 1 year in a slum area, in Kampung Sawah Jakarta. And one thing came straight to my mind: how am I going to survive in the local community? What will end up on my plate? Goodbye cheese, baguette and croissant.

Getting street food in the community immediately got my attention. On my first day, I walked around and discovered plenty of different colorful foods and smells — intriguing! Many different shops and restaurants every 5 meters. It looks like there is a lot of meat. Lots of oil. Everything looks fried. People look at me with questioning eyes, they call foreigners *bule* here. *"What is a bule doing here"*?

But I knew it was the beginning of my food journey in Jakarta — seeking to immerse myself in the community, something that spoke of the real

Indonesia. The first thing I tried is Nasi Goreng: probably the most famous meal in Indonesia. It is mainly rice with a little bit of meat, onion and vegetables and Sambal. Sambal? Indonesian chili sauce. Apparently Indonesian food is so spicy. *"It's okay, I put spicy sauce on my pizzas in France."* Yes. It's not okay. A tear fell down on my cheek. They are not kidding on this, but the taste was actually so good. People of the kampung were watching me with curiosity — do you like to eat spicy mister?

After this, I did not stop. Through sport playing with the kids and eating food in the community, I started slowly to integrate myself. They knew my name. They knew what I was doing here with LP4Y. Real smiles started to appear when they met me. And I went for it: Bakso (basically meatball), Saté (chicken with peanut sauce that can be considered as the national dish in Indonesia — I love it!), Nasi Padang, Nasi Bebek, Rendang, Indomie, different kinds of soups. Mostly with meat. It is quite complicated to be vegetarian.

It would be too long for me to describe everything to you, I just ended up really surprised that I almost loved it all. After months exploring the food, I was full. But my heart was even fuller. The warmth of the food, combined with the kindness of the people, made me feel like I had truly discovered something special. I knew that I was at the right place, fighting against

Youth exclusion in Jakarta. It was the kind of job and country I had come to find, not just in the food, but in the heart of its people.

CHAPTER REFLECTION

Reflect on a time when being part of a community made a significant difference in your life.

How did this sense of solidarity affect you and your situation?

CHAPTER 4: DREAMING BEYOND

The horizon of possibility extends far beyond the limits of the present. In this chapter, we delve into the ambitious dreams and visionary goals of LP4Y and the young people who are striving for a future that surpasses current constraints. This chapter is a celebration of the boundless potential within each individual, featuring stories of those who dare to dream of a world brimming with opportunities. Through their visionary aspirations, we are reminded that the future is full of infinite possibilities. By daring to dream beyond the confinements of today, we lay the foundation for a brighter and more hopeful tomorrow.

Just believe in yourself

Fadia Awad - STARS - Green Village Lebanon

I am Fadia, an Egyptian-Lebanese, residing in Lebanon, from the 28th batch of the GV Lebanon. I am currently 26 years old. I graduated in special education for people with special needs. Initially, I always wanted to be self-reliant, financially independent, and feel important in this society, but my studies were suspended for a period due to bad circumstances, and I was not a social person. I always isolated myself and hid behind everyone. My journey was not easy. I went through many, many crises and obstacles, fear, stress, poor living conditions, early responsibilities, and many other things. I was thinking that I was a person who does not change and that I was not good for anything. In the middle of my depression, I came across LP4Y on Instagram and loved the concept. I felt that they had read my dreams and that it was the place where I would start a new beginning away from the boredom of those who discouraged me, the first of whom being my parents. I applied and I was not expecting much, but they surprised me by contacting me and accepting me to join. I was very happy as if I had seen Hope for a better life.

With a lot of fear, tension, and astonishment I joined the Green Village. I was there for 3 months and it was the most beautiful experience I had ever lived. The Catalysts were very kind with their encouraging reception and support for us in all our steps during the most tough times.

All the young women, Coaches and beautiful leaders at LP4Y trusted us and taught us everything they could. Now, I am an independent woman financially and in life. I do not hide behind anyone. My voice is heard and my looks are sharp, and I know my abilities. I know that I CAN. All of you can never lose hope, there is always an opportunity waiting for you.

I hope to be able to travel and work abroad in the field of specialized education with a good job contract. I am strongly looking forward to that and I am trying to work hard to achieve it now. This is my dream. In the distant future, after I gain sufficient experience in life and work, I also aspire to work in the Life Project 4 Youth, which is currently being opened in Egypt.

Building hope through the Little Angels Academies

Marion Laurin - Project Manager LAA - India

After a shift from business to social work and numerous volunteer engagements in France and abroad for children's causes, I now find myself working with LP4Y to coordinate their 3 Little Angels Academies (LAA), which are nurseries.

From the start, my enthusiasm for this project was evident. As I told John, the founder of LP4Y, "*It's the LAAs or nothing!*" His response was just what I hoped for: "*OK Marion, the LAAs are a project dear to the Catalysts, and we need help to get it back on its feet!*" Challenge accepted!

The LAAs are one of the many innovative initiatives of LP4Y. As 85% of the Youth supported by LP4Y are young women, often young mothers, it was therefore obvious they needed help to take care of their children while following the LP4Y program. The goal is to enable these mothers to focus on their training and find decent work so they can offer a better life to their children.

For me, education is the starting point for a successful adult life. My ambition is to make the LAAs a place where every child has the opportunity to get a good start in life. In these nurseries, we don't just welcome the children of excluded young mothers; we offer them a safe environment where they can play, learn, thrive through various activities, and receive healthy meals. Each month, a medical check-up is organized to ensure everything is going well, as health problems in slums are numerous: malnutrition, pollution, unsanitary conditions. We also organize monthly excursions so the children can experience activities outside the slums — things their parents couldn't afford.

Though I am extremely motivated, the task is immense. The LAAs are located in three different countries: one in Kathmandu, Nepal; one in Tondo,

Manila in the Philippines; and one in Chennai, India, where I'm based. Six LAA Catalysts are responsible for the daily care of the children in these nurseries. My role is to ensure everything runs smoothly, despite the unique challenges of each location.

In Chennai, when I first took on the role, the situation was tough. Children were often half-naked because diapers were too expensive, their hair was messed up and infested with lice, and their little milk teeth were full of cavities. But despite these difficulties, their welcome was warm, full of laughter and smiles. I still remember Sham, a baby who was crying. Without hesitation, they put him in my arms, and before I knew it, his chocolate-covered mouth had stained my white t-shirt! Not the smartest choice of outfit, but I was there, finally on the field for a social mission; a lifelong goal realized. With a lot of work, things improved. The white walls of the LAA are now colorful with the children's drawings, and thanks to the awareness sessions for mothers led by the LAA Catalysts, chocolate and junk food have been replaced by healthier snacks. With the medical check-up, the children were sent to the dentist.

In the Philippines, another challenge awaited me. When I arrived at the LAA, I discovered that we had more cockroaches than children! The children did not seem bothered, playing hide-and-seek with them; a scene that, while common in the Philippines (I even saw street children walking cockroaches on leashes!), was not acceptable. It was clear the building was becoming unsanitary. My priority was to find a new place. In less than two months, we moved to a new location, thanks to the incredible commitment of the LAA Catalysts; Mariechu, Anabelle and her husband. It was not easy; my Birkenstocks still carry the memory of the white paint we used to repaint the walls! Today, the children are in a much healthier environment.

In Nepal, the situation is different. The challenges are fewer, but managing a large number of young children remains a demanding task.

The Little Angels Academies are much more than just a project for me. They represent a mission that deeply inspires me and pushes me to get up every morning with enthusiasm. These nurseries offer the children of marginalized mothers a space where they can flourish, learn, and grow safely. The LAAs are a bridge to a future where exclusion has no place, where every child, no matter where they come from, has the right to a good start in life.

What will happen to my future?

Tway Tar La Min - Youth - Yangon, Myanmar

My name is Tway Tar La Min. I am 23 years old and I am in the Management step in the Myanmar, Yangon, Hlaing Thar Yar LP4Y program.

When I learned that the center was closing because of the lockdown, it was unthinkable for me, I thought *"What will happen to my future?"*

During the lockdown, I attended Covid-19 Virus Volunteer Program, Hlaing Thar Yar Youths network. At home, I had the responsibility of cooking, washing and cleaning the house. I also followed LP4Y digital training. During this period, I missed Hlaing Thar Yar LP4Y center, hearing my friends laughing and having lunch together with my Coaches.

When the center opened again, my feeling was so great, I could not wait to see my Coaches and friends again. After the reopening we started doing micro-company work by department, digital training and volunteer time. The Youth could come to the center. Some Youth were doing computer training, some Youth were doing center renovation in small groups!

For me, LP4Y is a place where I can explore my dream. LP4Y is important for me because before LP4Y I was asking myself *"Who am I? What do I like and don't like? What are my skills, my abilities and my hobbies?"* LP4Y made me discover who I really am, what I want, and most of all, LP4Y gives me an opportunity. That is why LP4Y is important to me.

At LP4Y, I am working on my Life Project Plan. After LP4Y, I will find a decent job and improve step by step, so I will follow my dream which is to open my own shop. After I get my first job I plan to save money in order to buy a place where I can set up my clothes shop. I am still working on it. First, thanks to my Life

Project Plan book, I learned how to look for a job, what I need to know and which skills I need to reach my dream job.

We also have some guidance training, which allows me to think about my personal development. The IT training helps me to work on my resume and to send a professional email to apply for a job.

Thanks to LP4Y and our partners, we can do mock interviews. I was lucky to do one with the CCI (French Chamber of Commerce and Industry in Myanmar). It was my first English interview. I felt very stressed but in the end I was so happy because Pascaline Griffon (Business and Marketing Manager at CCI France Myanmar) told me she could help me to find a job. It was interesting to think about questions I didn't think about before. For example: imagine myself in 5 years or how to resolve problems with one of my teammates.

Would you hire me?

Josephlyn Palma - Catalyst - Manila, The Philippines

Let me start with a few questions:
Who here thinks a college degree is necessary? Who here has a job aligned with their degree? Who here already disqualified a candidate because they did not have a college degree?
Let me tell you: you are wrong.

Nowadays, out of 1.2 billion Youth, 700 million are coming from excluded backgrounds. Meaning that you will not include them in your recruitment process. That you would not include me, for example. And today, I will prove to you that you should have! The population is aging. Recruitment and talent retention are some of the main challenges HR will face in the future according to the ILO organization. So you should consider thinking outside of the box of Education and go FURTHER.

The preconceived idea of Youth being lazy, not willing to work or to take initiatives remains printed in our mind. But do you trust us enough? Do you give us enough opportunities to thrive? Do you use the right framework to accompany us?

I am telling you today that when you give an opportunity to a Youth coming from an excluded background, he or she will not give up. I will not give up.

We are responsible for our families, for our future. We are therefore committed and have the willingness to champion for your brand, your company. We are proud because this might be the first time someone believes in us. Fast learning, flexibility, and responsibility are not taught while sitting on a bench.

By hiring an excluded Youth, you will have access to a better workforce and you will also directly impact your image and the way people see your brand. You will reach your diversity objectives, which we know are a success indicator in terms of well-being, motivation and creativity for your employees. You will even enjoy tax deduction from your government! Amazing, right?

But you already know that.

Do you want to have an impact?
Do you want to follow the process or do you want to be the one leading the change?
Do you want to be a follower of the next champions of inclusion or do you want to be that Champion of inclusion?

Of course it can look complicated knowing where to start. Today, I will share with you a few tips on how to have an impact starting tomorrow:
Contact the Youth Inclusion Network to shape your HR strategy and be connected to the Youth;
Remove educational requirements in all your job offers;
Support financially Youth inclusion initiatives;
Be a speaker during events to inspire and be a role model for many more organizations;

Raise awareness around you: you are part of the change!

Excluded Youth are full of skills, dreams and talents. They are eager to join you, they are eager to show you who they really are and I am one of these Youths. I have skills, I have potential and I deserve that chance.

Let me show you what I can bring. Beyond the data in your HR records, we are talking about loyalty, willingness to learn and so much more.

Diplomas will never bring the practical experience that I gained throughout my life, while struggling to succeed. Today, I am able to bring so much more than a piece of paper at an interview. I bring you 21 years of practical experience that will definitely change the way you will perceive interviews and candidates. I am bringing you a new field of possibilities, full of talents that deserve to be discovered.
I am Josephlyn and I am the one who can open you to this world.
And now, would you hire me?

My wave of Dreams (मेरा सपनाका लहरहरु)

Yog Maya Sunuwar - Entrepreneur - Kathmandu, Nepal

I was born in a beautiful holy village at the foot of green hills, beautiful mountains. It has been almost 2 years since I started living in the city. Today, I am writing this, my story, myself, I am writing to find memories of my past.

I am Yog Maya Sunuwar from Ramechhap district, Nepal and nowadays I'm in Kathmandu city. I am 21 years old and I'm studying for a Bachelor's degree.

I came to the city for my studies and I'm seeking a decent job for my financial freedom and to complete my degree. I searched many places but I didn't find a job. In this time, I met many fraudulent companies which would ask me to pay to get a job. I lost some of my money and lots of time to search for a job. I was fully tired. When I found a job, they would also ask me for experience but I never had a job before. I only found a few decent jobs.

One day, my friend posted on Facebook about LP4Y providing different types of training for women only. After receiving these, I decide to go there and understand what's happening there, what types of training they provide. I went there and saw many ladies, all speaking English. And I saw that all were very educated and also talented. I thought: *"Oh my God! I came from a government school and I'm not good at English."* I felt bad about myself, but sometime later, one lady came and told me that in fact, when they came there, they also didn't know about English. After learning there, they are able to speak English and understand English. After listening to their inspiring and motivational stories, I decided to join this organization.

I saw there are many foreigners working in this organization and I thought, if there are foreigners, my English will also improve. Because I need to speak in English there. So that's why I decided to join. There are many foreign Catalysts who help us to develop ourselves. We have two Coaches who teach us about professionalism, English, and mainly education. So, I am very inspired and quickly I joined this.

The second day, finally, I joined this organization and on this day, I see all the Youth are very helpful and they all teach us about their organization. Apart from the skills, I learned there that this training is for every woman who wants to become independent in their life. There are lots of women like me who want to become independent.

There I also work at different types of departments because we manage a micro-company that provides computer training for community people. So, I worked during 6 months of my training in different types of departments like Human Resources, Communication and Marketing, Ecosystem Development, and Learning and Development. Firstly, I started in the Communication and Marketing department. I saw the Coaches (Albrina Singh and Shreya Baral) were very friendly and helpful because they helped me a lot. They told us *"If you have any questions, curiosity, if you have any problem, please share with us."* And also during my training, if I got a problem and confusion, I went to them for help and they helped me anytime.

During my training time, there were many events that happened, many guests were coming there. I also attended many events as a host, and I also worked in a team, or as a team leader that time. We did many tasks and projects. I got a chance to visit with our national and international visiting places, like

Bouddha, Patan temples, Pashupatinath Mandir, with many foreigners. I got a chance to interact with people from so many different countries and I loved working with people with different personalities. I developed my education, my mindset, my personality, my English speaking skills, my computer skills in speed, management, decision making, and problem solving. I developed a lot, a lot in this organization. During this training time, I found myself. So thank you so much Life Project 4 Youth training program. I am always thankful for you.

Now, I am able to think about my short term and long term goals. Before that I only thought that I would first complete my study and only focused on that, but after this training, I made plans on how to reach my short term goal (Content Editor) to long term goal (Opening my own business).

The Catalysts and Coaches always inspired us to follow our own dreams. They are my heroes because I want to become independent and helpful like them. I am always thankful for the Life Project 4 Youth.
Finally, I completed my six month professional training at the organization. That was a special memory for me. After finishing this training I also found a decent job in Kalpavrikshya Education Foundation as a Content Editor. I'm very excited for the new job but I'm sad for leaving the organization, because during training we are all like family there.

I tell myself that, "*Hey, be happy with changes in what's happening in your life because everything gives you lessons. You need to accept that and move forward. Success is waiting for you. Let's move!"*

Lastly, I want to say thank you so much Life Project 4 Youth for your support and help. Without your support and help, I am not able to become what I am today. Today, I am clear about my goal, vision, and also my field of interest. So, thank you so much Coaches, Catalysts, all the Youth and Life Project 4 Youth for making my journey wonderful and developing myself. Thank you so much!

---

18 months after Graduating from LP4Y

Yair Lynn Naing - STARS – Myanmar

My name is Yair Lynn Naing. I live in Hlaing Thar Yar Tsp. I am part of LP4Y STARS club (alumni from LP4Y program) and I am working in CMA Ships Myanmar as an administrative officer.

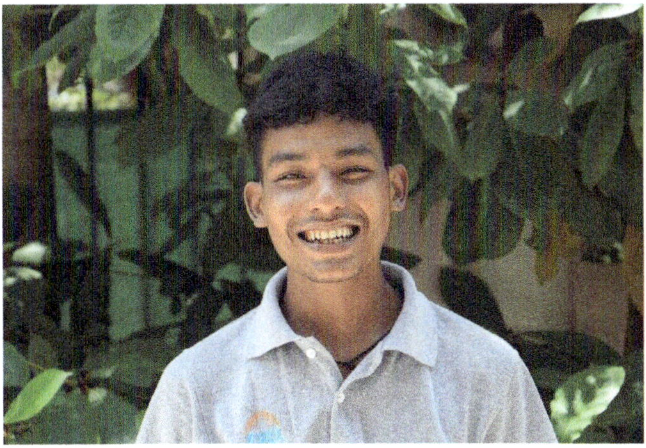

Here is my story from LP4Y to CMA: how did I join LP4Y? How did LP4Y help me to get a job? Before I joined LP4Y, I was a worker in a market and it was very tiring. I did not want to work in that job. I wanted to work somewhere where I can improve my life.

One day, a woman came and informed my mom I could join LP4Y, explaining that it is an organization helping excluded Youth living in poor areas. I am very grateful that my Mom allowed me to quit my previous job and join LP4Y.

When I joined LP4Y, the training center was in a monastery in Hlaing Thar Yar. For 9 months, I went to LP4Y center every day from Tuesday to Saturday, learning and working on our small business. LP4Y gave us allowance for breakfast, lunch, dinner, water, hygiene products, professional attire and mobile phone. Thanks for donating LP4Y!

LP4Y also helped me to learn how to write a cover letter and resumé. I did not know how to write it before. After 2 months in LP4Y, I went to CMA Ships Myanmar for a 10-day internship. I finished the LP4Y program during the COVID pandemic and started searching for a decent job.

During COVID, even if we could not open our center, LP4Y continued to train Youth through video conferencing. I am very grateful for that because if the program had stopped, I would have not been able to find a job.

For almost two years, I worked in other companies, hoping that CMA Ships would hire me. And I finally got a job! I still remember the day the manager in CMA called me and said: "*Hello Yair Lynn, when can you start to work in our company?*" I was so happy to hear that.

I started my job at CMA Ships on April 1, 2022. The employees are professional, confident, hardworking, patient, and also good at English. I learned these skills from them. The management of CMA is one of the best I ever experienced. I am so happy to work there because that was my target job. There is no discrimination or corruption in CMA. While working here, I am learning English step by step. Getting better is my challenge now!

Thank you LP4Y and donors for helping the poor Youth in Myanmar when we are hopeless.

Together We Can!

Working with the Youth: Bringing a new vibe

Ludovic Bouvier - ID Logistics - Jakarta, Indonesia

At LP4Y, we believe that together we can reach a brighter future and work together towards Youth inclusion. We say that the Catalysts are building the bridge between the integrated and excluded world. After a first approach and visit to TDC Jakarta by Ludovic Bouvier from ID Logistics and his team, we realized that we were willing to overcome the same challenges in helping excluded Youths. On this day, we decided on both sides, to put the first foundation of this bridge and start working together for the same cause.

My name is Ludovic Bouvier. I am the Director of ID Logistics in Indonesia. Our company is deeply committed to values like solidarity and entrepreneurship. We believe that being a good employee, and even more importantly a good human being, comes from a willingness to do better, to always move forward and to learn from others. In ID Logistics, Inclusivity has always been part of our company values. We are a company providing logistics services thus our people, our know-how is key to our strategy.

End of 2023, together with the LP4Y team we elaborated a collaboration aiming at helping excluded Youths. At ID Logistics, we share a similar mission of providing equal opportunities, especially for young people. We saw this partnership as a chance to support the Youth in developing their skills and improving their chances of not just finding employment, but also securing decent jobs in the future.

What particularly resonated with me was LP4Y's approach — they were not just asking for financial support, but for a tangible, hands-on way to contribute to these young people's lives. I was particularly impressed by the professionalism of the LP4Y volunteers and the global training pedagogy for the Youths. "Learning by doing" - that is what they told us on our arrival. And step by step, we really saw what it meant. I thought the pedagogy was really innovative, adapted to the environment, and the main thing was to support the Youths to have a positive and professional behavior.

Together with the ID Logistics team, we truly believe and want to involve ourselves in projects that have a real long-term impact and human dimension. This is what we found at LP4Y and made us willing to be part of this ecosystem.

When we first visited the LP4Y center, the team was surprised by the differences in life experiences. They quickly understood the situation and decided to be a driving force in this adventure. Thus, we decided to integrate Youth interns from LP4Y into our team, not as mere interns but as colleagues. Currently, we have three Youths (1 Youth in ID Logistics office and 2 Youths working in ID Logistics warehouse) who are working closely with our employees. The goal is to immerse them fully into the working environment, so they do not just gain skills but also experience working with people from diverse backgrounds. The global feedback from the team is that they are so happy with the Youths' job so far!

What drives me to give these opportunities to the Youths of LP4Y is the spirit of education in a tangible way. I believe in giving young people, especially those from disadvantaged areas, the chance to prove themselves. The most important thing we can do is train them, show them different environments and rules to have a positive mindset and to continuously learn — qualities that LP4Y emphasizes. Their potential is strong and we want to help them raise and find it.

So far, the integration has been very positive. Our employees have embraced the interns as part of the team. They are not just treating them as temporary workers but as colleagues who are here to learn and contribute. This has created a more inclusive environment and brought fresh perspectives to our team. The Youths bring a different energy, and it has been a learning experience for everyone involved.
My hope is that after their training, the Youths doing their internship at ID Logistics will be well-equipped to find stable jobs and continue to grow in their careers.

I expect that they will leave ID Logistics not just with skills but with a positive mindset and the confidence to pursue their goals. It is not just about the immediate impact, we wish to set them on a path toward a brighter future.

To other companies considering similar initiatives, I would say: Don't hesitate! It is our duty as companies to contribute and prepare the next generation. This is not about charity, it is about creating real opportunities and building a more inclusive society. Engaging in projects like this is not only beneficial for the Youth but also for the company, as it brings fresh perspectives and energy to the workplace and teams. It is important to give back some of what we have for a more balanced environment. My only expectation is that the interns we work with will be able to find stable jobs thanks to our shared moment together. Nothing more. I wish this support given by ID Logistics could mean something for the Youths' life.

Our fruitful interactions with the Youths

Pascaline Griffon - Head of Business services CCI France, Myanmar

My name is Pascaline Griffon, I am Head of Business Services at CCI France Myanmar. At the French Myanmar Chamber of Commerce & Industry (FMCCI), our objectives are to support the development of our members (French, Myanmar and international companies), to help foreign companies settle in Myanmar and to develop economic relations between France and Myanmar.

The LP4Y team came to us in 2019 to explain their project and to see how we could collaborate. At FMCCI, we strongly believe in equal opportunities, we think that it is also part of our objectives to help the Youth, to develop their skills and to improve their chance to have access not only to employment but also to fulfilling jobs. LP4Y gave us a chance to enhance our work on those matters.
With more than 150 members, FMCCI is a great way to spread information and awareness about LP4Y. Therefore, we sent an email to our network to present the association and give our members the opportunity to contribute to this remarkable project.

In addition, we have organized a visit to the FMCCI office for the Youth, during which FMCCI team members (including myself) made presentations in relation to our respective jobs to give the Youth some useful tips and information about recruitment, management, and marketing. After that, the Youth presented us with their micro-company projects. It was a great learning experience for both sides, and we intend to renew it as soon as the situation allows us to welcome visitors again.

Following my presentation on how to prepare a CV, a cover letter, and a job interview, I decided to volunteer on a personal basis on weekends to help the Youth in their job search mainly by training them for job interviews. Besides preparing them, mock interviews are always a great occasion to discuss their professional projects, to see if there could be any opportunity with CCI France Myanmar's members. Indeed, FMCCI is a good networking platform for job research and some of our members are already invested in LP4Y by offering the Youth internships or jobs opportunities within their companies.

CCI France Myanmar has a strong focus on HR support, so we plan to develop a win-win collaboration that could be beneficial for both LP4Y and our members.

Vocational training to complement my (as yet) unfinished formal education

Ahmad - Youth - Jakarta, Indonesia

My name is Ahmad, from Indonesia. A little introduction about myself: I lived in Kampung Sawah, Jakarta, Indonesia without family support which meant I had to work part-time to afford basic necessities and school fees. It wasn't easy, and eventually, I had to make the difficult decision to leave formal education. It was the time when I found *Balai Latihan Kerja,* or the Training and Development Center in English, from my friend and decided to join. However, my journey took a turn when I discovered LP4Y. This professional training institution became my new home, where I not only learned practical skills for the workplace but also gained a deeper understanding of the waiting process and teamwork. LP4Y wasn't just an educational institution; it became a family to me, filled with supportive friends and mentors who believed in my potential.

I have no junior high school friends anymore but I found friends in LP4Y.

Through working on my Life Project Plan, I began to see a path forward. It wasn't just about surviving day-to-day anymore; I started dreaming again. At LP4Y, I do not need a school uniform to learn English. I am not enrolled in a formal school, but I am getting more than a school can give.

Now, I am on an internship at ID Logistics, where I apply everything I learned during micro-company Care 4 Change: managing administrative tasks, handling Youth allowances, creating informative brochures. During my internship in ID Logistics, I had to take responsibilities, such as when I am handling micro-company (MC) tasks at LP4Y. For example, we need to take responsibility every time our water gallon is empty at LP4Y center or every time there is a complaint about the training. We also learn about communication within a team. Now I can practice with my clients in the workplace.

Last, I always remember the Coach support and I decided to pursue my high school equivalency (Package C) using the earnings from my internship. This decision not only empowered me but also solidified my determination to create a better future for myself.

Being a teacher is my greatest show!

Alifa Salsabila Sari - STARS - Surabaya, Indonesia

Within half a month after finishing training at LP4Y, I found a new job and was accepted at a school where I became a teacher. The feeling was incredibly mixed and overwhelming as I secured a job that matched my skills. However, every job has its pros and cons. As a teacher, my salary might not be as high as at my previous company, but that's not a reason to doubt success, right? Success is not just about salary; it's about how you can achieve your dreams and aspirations for good and meaningful purposes. I actually just knew about a decent job because of LP4Y and at LP4Y, I came to understand that by improving my skills, I have come to love my current job.

At LP4Y, many aspects of myself have improved, especially skills I never knew I had. At LP4Y, I felt that I was in a place where everything needed to be tried and done without fear of starting, particularly when it comes to education. Education is a primary option that must always be pursued. One extraordinary thing I discovered was teaching. In my life, I had

never considered teaching, and this has been an incredibly amazing new experience.
From this experience, I have come to love teaching because it allows us to learn many things we never thought of before. I have come to understand the character of children, learned to balance my emotions, and grasped the true meaning of dedication. Now for me, success is when I can pursue my dream as a teacher, happy and enjoying being an impact for my personal growth and for my nation.

My messages to all the Youth out there: seize the good opportunities within you while you are young. You deserve a job that aligns with your dreams. Be enthusiastic and seek experiences and self-improvement at LP4Y, which will provide the facilities and support to help you become extraordinary. Thank you, LP4Y, for helping me find a job that suits my personality.

The Rise of Easy Fruits Pvt. Ltd. & Collaboration with LP4Y Nepal

Preety Sigdel - Founder - Easy Fruits PVT. LTD - Nepal

In a fast-paced world where convenience often trumps nutrition, Easy Fruits Pvt. Ltd. has emerged as a pioneering force in Nepal, making fruit eating accessible, hassle-free, and sustainable. Founded by a visionary entrepreneur, Easy Fruits aimed to revolutionize the way people consumed fresh produce.

Based in Kathmandu, Nepal, this innovative company has taken the concept of fresh fruit delivery to a new level, offering a unique subscription service that ensures customers enjoy a steady supply of fresh, ready-to-eat fruits and fresh juice without any of the usual preparation time. The company's mission was simple yet profound: to make high-quality, fresh fruits accessible and convenient for everyone.

The concept of Easy Fruits originated as a project for an MBA thesis. The founder, Preety Sigdel, while pursuing her degree, was inspired by the complexities and inefficiencies in the fresh produce supply chain. She noticed how many people struggled to find fresh, affordable fruit and saw an opportunity to address this gap. At the time, Preety was working in a senior position at Save The Children Nepal, a global NGO, where she witnessed first-hand the impact of food insecurity on communities. Preety was determined to address this problem, and her thesis laid the groundwork for what would become Easy Fruits.

Preety, who is passionate about healthy living and deeply concerned with hygiene and nutrition, put her academic research into practice. She decided to create a service that would deliver farm-fresh fruits directly to people's doorsteps, combining her business acumen with a commitment to health and wellness. Additionally, she envisioned Easy Fruits as an all-female enterprise, emphasizing female empowerment and creating opportunities for women in the workforce. The company's first employee was an LP4Y graduate. LP4Y had a significant presence in Nepal, empowering Youth through education, training, and community support initiatives.

In the early days, Easy Fruits faced numerous challenges especially in markets where the concept is relatively new. It took us four months to find our first female driver for delivery. Due to societal norms and gender rules, female delivery drivers are rare. In Nepal, traditional gender roles often dictate that women should prioritize domestic responsibilities over professional careers, particularly those that involve physical labor or non-traditional roles like driving. This societal expectation limits the number of women who pursue jobs as drivers. However, Preety's unwavering dedication and innovative thinking, honed during her MBA and her experience at Save The Children, led to the development of a unique business model. Easy Fruit partnered with LP4Y Nepal to create opportunities and support systems for young women entering the workforce.

This partnership not only helped Easy Fruits address the gender disparity in the workforce, but also contributed to breaking societal barriers by offering women a chance to prove their capabilities. Through such collaborations, Easy Fruits demonstrated its commitment to fostering an inclusive work environment and supporting community development by empowering marginalized groups, particularly women, to participate in the workforce.

Beyond recruitment, Easy Fruits has actively engaged with LP4Y through various initiatives and events. We have participated in Youth Inclusion Network (YIN) and Youth 4 Change Network (Y4CN) events, where our representatives have not only attended but also contributed as panelists during discussions on Youth employment. Our involvement has extended to organizing mock interviews, where we have provided practical feedback to LP4Y trainees, and impact meetings, where we have shared insights and best practices.

Furthermore, Easy Fruits has had the honor of inviting LP4Y Youth and Catalysts for company visits, offering them a firsthand look at our operations and providing mentorship opportunities. We have also proudly participated in LP4Y's campaign during Women's Month, celebrating and advocating for the empowerment of young women in the workforce. Additionally, we have testified about our successful collaboration with LP4Y during the Monitoring and Evaluation (MAE) process, underscoring the tangible benefits and positive outcomes of this partnership.

This initiative also aligns with the broader goals of LP4Y, which focuses on equipping young women with skills and opportunities that enable them to achieve economic independence and build sustainable careers. As the company grew, so did its offerings. Easy Fruits expanded its range to include fresh fruit, fresh cut fruit as snacks, fresh fruit juice and fruit baskets for special occasions, and even fruit subscription boxes for those who wanted a regular supply of their favorite fruits. They also introduced a recycling program for their packaging, reinforcing their commitment to sustainability.

Through its journey, Easy Fruits never lost sight of its core values: quality, convenience, community, hygiene, nutrition, and female empowerment. The company continues to partner with LP4Y, innovate and adapt, always striving to meet the evolving needs of its customers. Easy Fruits' story is a testament to the power of passion and perseverance in creating a business that not only thrives but also makes a positive impact on society. It became more than just a company; it became a symbol of healthy living, community support, female empowerment, and a brighter, fruit-filled future for all, proving that a well-thought-out MBA thesis, experience in a global NGO, and a strong commitment to hygiene and nutrition can indeed change the world.

CHAPTER REFLECTION

Success looks different though every set of eyes.

What does it look like for you in relation to your dreams?

CONCLUSION

As we reach the end of our journey, picture the sky once more, with a broader view. The individual lights of each story blend together, creating a mesmerizing constellation that lights up the night. Our guiding star, once a symbol of one person's journey — now merges with countless others, forming a magnificent array of shared dreams and achievements.

In this map of stars, each one represents a unique journey, a personal triumph and a shared vision of a brighter tomorrow. The sky above us is no longer a void, but a canvas painted with the light of resilience, ambition, community and boundless dreams. As you close this book, remember that you too are a part of this celestial tapestry, a star whose light contributes to the grandeur of our shared universe. Together, we illuminate the path forward, inspiring each other to push beyond today's realities and strive for the dreams of tomorrow.

Together, We Can!

LP4Y GLOSSARY

As language is part of the change we want to induce, LP4Y developed its terminology to strengthen its message.

LP4Y: an international movement or organization rather than an NGO, a foundation, or an association. LP4Y Alliance gathers independent entities registered upon different statuses depending on the country of implementation.

Youth: To refer to the young people LP4Y accompanies

Catalysts: To refer to LP4Y team members, symbolizing a reaction provoking change

Training and Development Center (TDC): Located close to slums, the TDC are the places where LP4Y accompany the Youth towards their professional and social inclusion through a 6-month program. It is also the place where Catalysts live.

Green Village (GV): Located in rural areas, GV are the places where we accompany the Youth toward their professional and social inclusion through a 3-month program. This residential program focuses on sustainability.

Life Project Money (LPM): weekly allowance provided to the Youth to enable them to follow the training (covers transportation fees, professional attire, hygiene expenses).

Micro Company (MC): Professionalizing, based on learning by doing/learning by experiencing a pedagogical tool that allows the Youth to have a positive first professional experience while gaining critical interpersonal skills. Through this Micro Company, the Youth provide training adapted to each local community's needs about health topics (hygiene, nutrition, menstruation awareness), sports, computer & English basic knowledge, and access to decent employment.

Life Project Plan (LPP): Youth explore their LPP throughout their time in the program to discover, enhance or gain insight on their dreams and ambitions in a realistic and achievable way.

STARS: an LP4Y acronym for share, train, act, reach & support. It is the title given to Youth after completing the program. They automatically become a part of this club after graduation. It is designed as a network to enhance the integration process and encourages togetherness.

Little Angels Academies (LAA): nurseries settled in the Training and Development Centers to welcome the children of the young mothers following LP4Y programs. It contributes to the education and development of children through training in hygiene, nutrition, health, safety and child development.

Professional Training Program (PTE): Used to refer to the 3 to 6 month unique pedagogy training used and developed by LP4Y.

Printed by Amazon Italia Logistica S.r.l.
Torrazza Piemonte (TO), Italy

63387624R00100